If Walls Could Talk:

Chapala's historic buildings
and their former occupants

Burton, Tony, 1953-, author
    If Walls Could Talk: Chapala's historic buildings and their former
occupants
/ Tony Burton.

Includes maps, notes, bibliographical references and index.
ISBN 978-1-7770381-4-4 (paperback)
ISBN 978-1-7770381-5-1 (Ebook)

ISBN 978-1-7770381-4-4
First edition 2020
Text and cartography © 2020 by Tony Burton
Cover image: detail from a photograph by Winfield Scott, colorized and
published as a postcard c. 1905 by J. Granat, Mexico City.

Sombrero Books, Box 4, Ladysmith B.C. V9G 1A1, Canada

If Walls Could Talk:

Chapala's historic buildings and their former occupants

TONY BURTON

SB

SOMBRERO BOOKS, B.C., CANADA

Contents

PART C: East of the pier

Maps

Text boxes

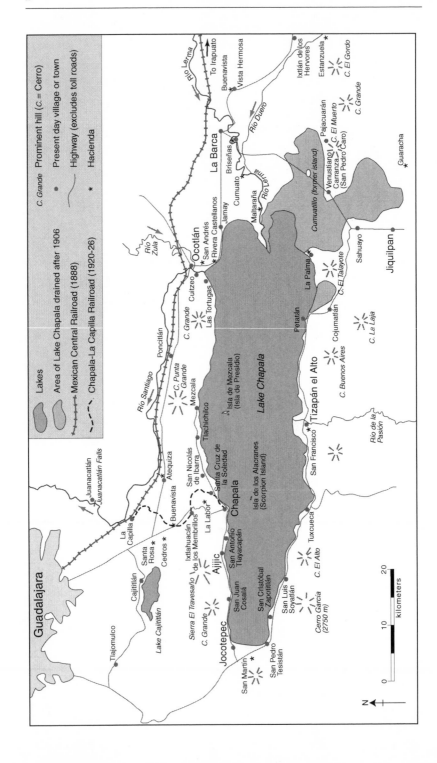

Preface

Lake Chapala played an important role in the history of tourism in North America and is now recognized as one of the world's premier retirement destinations. Yet, the details of how and why this transformation occurred have never been adequately reconstructed.

Frustrated at reading accounts of the area that repeat long-standing errors and half-truths, I have been systematically trying to unravel Chapala's rich and extraordinary history for more than two decades.

Join me on a walking tour of Chapala and explore the history of its formative years as I share the remarkable and revealing stories attached to its many historic buildings and their former residents.

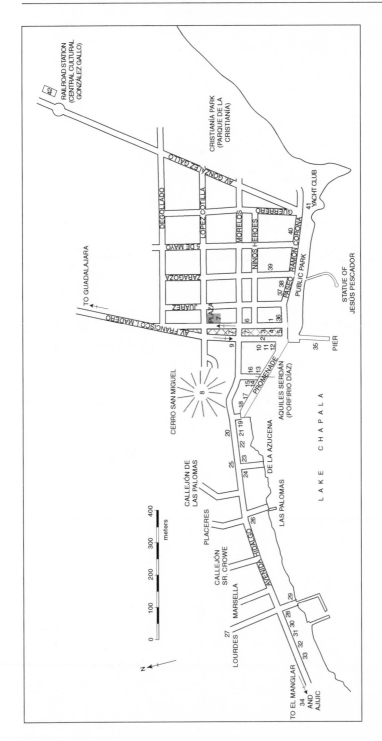

Street Plan of Chapala today. Numbers correspond to chapters in this book.

Introduction

Chapala's rise to international prominence

This book looks at how Chapala, a small nondescript fishing village in Jalisco, suddenly shot to international prominence at the end of the nineteenth century as one of North America's earliest tourist resorts. Within twenty years, Chapala, tucked up against the hills embracing the northern shore of Mexico's largest natural lake, was attracting the cream of Mexican and foreign society. Thus began Lake Chapala's astonishing transformation into the vibrant international community it is now, so beloved of authors, artists and retirees.

My focus is on the stories of the town's historic buildings, many of them still standing today, and of their former residents. The numerous fine old homes, hotels and other buildings from the first half of the twentieth century have given Chapala an immensely rich cultural legacy that deserves to be both revered and preserved.

Organized as a walking tour, the book covers not only existing buildings but also some significant early buildings that no longer exist. It is only a partial guide to the town's many historic buildings; an inventory prepared by the National Institute of Anthropology and History identified more than eighty such buildings in Chapala. Some of the more interesting properties are not easily visible from the road; they are hidden behind high walls and better viewed from the lake.

The book is divided into three parts. Starting at the main church, Part A (chapters 1 to 18) considers the central, downtown area of Chapala and the short promenade west of the pier. Part B (chapters 19 to 34) looks at some of the numerous villas lining Avenida Hidalgo to the westernmost outskirts of Chapala. Part C (chapters 35 to 42) starts at the pier and heads east; it includes the villas that lined the former beach

(Chacaltita) as far as Chapala Yacht Club and concludes at the Chapala
Railroad Station, now the Centro Cultural González Gallo.

An Englishman and his dreams

But when and how did Chapala's rise to fame begin? After visiting
the village in July 1892, American Thomas Rogers had presciently remarked how,

> Chapala is sure to become more and more a favorite watering place.
> Already there are some fine summer "seaside" cottages there, and
> in the offing you can see a yacht! With a combination of delightful
> climate and hot springs, with mountain climbing, boating, bathing,
> and fishing as recreations for visitors, why shouldn't charming Chapala
> become the finest health and pleasure resort in Mexico?[1]

The man credited with being the first outsider to settle in Chapala
was an eccentric Englishman named Septimus Crowe. We don't know
exactly when Crowe first visited Chapala, but he was certainly living at
the lake well before 1893, when Mexican diplomat-author Eduardo A.
Gibbon published this description:

> The very lovely estate that can be seen from the lake on a hill, a quarter
> of a league from the village of Chapala, is the work and property of
> an English gentleman, who with his love for Mexican nature, and a
> culture only proper for one of his education and social standing, has
> brought much life to this region, and has also stimulated others to
> build holiday homes and with them give life and civilization to this
> very beautiful region.[2]

That estate, now known as Villa Montecarlo, was built by Crowe.
Clearly, several other villas had already been constructed in Chapala by
that time; these included Villa Ana Victoria and Casa Capetillo.

In the remaining years of the nineteenth century, numerous other
villas, chalets and mansions were added. By the end of the century, the
village had its first modern hotel: the Hotel Arzapalo, which opened in
1898. During the first decade of the twentieth century, tourism was on the
rise and Chapala's population grew rapidly, from about 1750 inhabitants
in 1900 to 2200 by the end of the decade.

While the Mexican Revolution (1910–1920) brought a sharp de-
cline in tourism, the population of Chapala continued to grow rapidly as

people from the surrounding countryside sought the relative security of the lakeside town. Visitor numbers soon recovered, and grew steadily in succeeding decades, except for short periods during the Cristeros Rebellion (1926–1929) or when the regional economy was struggling.

Fortuitous presidential connection

Even if Septimus Crowe, who first recognized the allure of living on the lakeshore and even brought his own yacht to the lake, must be singled out for his role in this dramatic transformation of a small village into a modern tourist mecca, chance—in the form of two beautiful and intelligent young women—also played a part. Carmen Romero Rubio had married Mexico's despotic president, Porfirio Díaz, in 1881. Her sister, Sofía, was the wife of Lorenzo Elizaga, a wealthy Mexico City lawyer. At the start of the twentieth century the Elizagas built El Manglar, a vacation retreat reachable only by boat, a short distance west of Chapala.

President Díaz and his wife visited their in-laws in Chapala more than once, putting Chapala on the map as far as the upper echelons of Mexican society were concerned. Given the presidential seal of approval, members of the Mexico City elite, and of the less numerous Guadalajara elite, began a mad scramble to build their own homes at the lake.

Architects, building materials and costs

The earliest chalets, such as those erected by Septimus Crowe, are believed to have been imported wooden prefabricated buildings.[3] More substantial, architect-designed buildings quickly followed. Several of the early iconic buildings in Chapala that have survived to this day were designed or remodeled by foreign architects.

English architect George Edward King, responsible for several theaters in Mexico, designed both Villa Tlalocan (begun in 1895) and Casa Braniff (built 1904–05), and perhaps one or two others. Working with King was another English architect, Charles Grove Johnson. An American architect, Charles Lincoln Strange, may have designed Casa Paulsen (Villa Paz), while Italian architect Angelo Corsi built Villa Macedonia and remodeled Villa Montecarlo.

The most noteworthy Mexican architect in Chapala's early tourist years was Guillermo de Alba. De Alba, born in Mexico City, graduated as an engineer in Guadalajara and then spent some time in Chicago. He began his career in Chapala by working with Manuel Henríquez and building

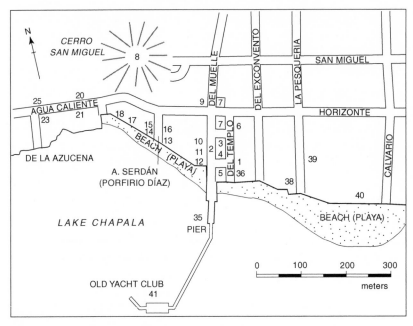

Street plan of Chapala in 1915, based on a map by Guillermo de Alba.
Numbers on both maps refer to chapters in this book.

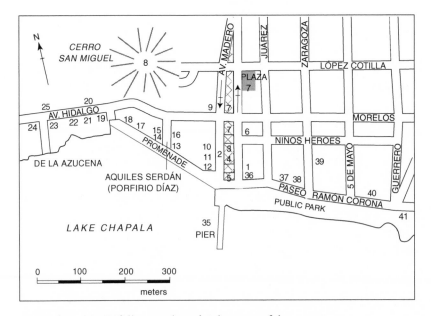

Street plan in 1951, following the redevelopment of the town center.

houses.[4] De Alba later designed his own family home (Mi Pullman), Hotel Palmera, Villa Niza and the Railroad Station, completed in 1920.

In 1898, after talking with de Alba, a newspaper correspondent reported that most homes were either stone or brick and that there were no wooden houses. Stone came from Atequiza (north of Chapala) or from Tizapán el Alto on the lake's southern shore. Bricks, costing "$11 to $12 per thousand," also came from across the lake.

A "comfortable cottage of eight or ten rooms, of two stories, built solidly with good foundations" cost $6,000 to $8,000. Land had become expensive: lakeshore lots sold for ninety cents a square meter, compared to three cents a meter a few years earlier. This inflation of land prices was "one of the signs of the modern times in Chapala."[5]

From the 1930s onwards, several modernist architects, most of them graduates of the Guadalajara engineering school, undertook projects in Chapala. By far the most famous was Luis Barragán, the greatest Mexican architect of the twentieth century, who redesigned his family home near the church, laid out his earliest garden at a property on Avenida Hidalgo, and reworked several other buildings. Other architects of note whose work in Chapala can still be admired include Pedro Castellanos Lambley, Juan Palomar y Arias and Ignacio Díaz Morales.[6]

Street plan and street names

Septimus Crowe and his cronies would not recognize Chapala today. The earliest street names in Chapala, approved in 1889 at about the time Crowe arrived, are now totally different.[7] The street plan today is also markedly different.

Prior to 1950, from Avenida Hidalgo south, two parallel streets— Calle del Muelle to the west and Calle del Templo (Calle del Atrio on some early maps) to the east—ran towards the lake; these streets helped define a small plaza (*jardín*) and a block of buildings. The *jardín* was relocated, and the buildings demolished, when the wide modern central avenue—Avenida Francisco I. Madero—that now leads to the pier was created in about 1950. Calle del Muelle became the west side of the avenue and Calle del Templo the east side.

The main route from Chapala to Ajijic, now Avenida Hidalgo, was formerly known as Calle del Agua Caliente, after the local hot springs. It was renamed on 16 September 1910 to coincide with Mexico's centenary celebrations. At the same time, five central streets were given cobblestones,

Chapala's first Palacio Municipal (Town Hall) was inaugurated, and the central plaza was smartened up and christened Jardín Hidalgo.[8]

The other streets in the center of Chapala also changed names a long time ago. Calle del Horizonte became Morelos; Calle de San Miguel became López Cotilla; and Calle de la Pesquería (where fishing nets were stretched out to dry) was renamed Zaragoza.

The parish church of San Francisco, c. 1900. (Ignacio Arzapalo)
The church, plastered white for much of its history, was covered with quarried stone (*cantera*) in the late 1960s.

Part A

1

Parish church of San Francisco

The principal church in Chapala (La Parroquia de San Francisco de Asís) was built in the mid-eighteenth century on the site of the town's first humble, adobe-walled church which had been founded in 1548 by Father Juan de Almolón. That church was burned down in 1557 by an indigenous man named Juan Tzincayol; its replacement was burned down by "Pablo, the son of Martín García," in 1581.[1]

When Father Sebastián de Párraga was assigned to the friary in Chapala in 1562, he arrived with the area's first orange trees, which he planted with the assistance of a fellow friar, Francisco Tenorio.

The most noteworthy of the many evangelizing friars who served this region was Italian-born Miguel de Bolonia. Born in about 1500, he was one of the first Franciscans to arrive in Mexico in 1524. He learned several indigenous languages and helped resettle groups of "Indians", following their conversion to Christianity, into new villages such as Chapala and Ajijic. Shortly after his death in the friary on 14 July 1580 a large comet appeared in the sky over Chapala. Father Miguel de Bolonia's innumerable contributions to Chapala are commemorated by an inscribed marble stone laid in 1943 in the presbytery of the church.[2]

The current neoclassic Parroquia had its bell towers added in the nineteenth century. An inscription in the southern tower suggests it was completed in 1878. Among the stonemasons responsible for these towers was Faustino Gil, who later created an unusual sculpture of a lioness out of the volcanic ash that fell on Chapala during the eruption of Colima Volcano in 1913.[3] The towers were the same height prior to the late 1960s, when the northern tower was left slightly higher following a partially-completed remodeling of the facade.

The clock above the church's main entrance was added in about 1897, at the time the Hotel Arzapalo was being built. The clock was a gift of Eduard Collignon, owner of the nearby Villa Ana Victoria.[4] At about the same time, a fence was added to define the boundaries of the atrium.

The imposing Parroquia gets several mentions in D. H. Lawrence's *The Plumed Serpent*.[5] The church was only a short stroll from the house Lawrence rented in Chapala while composing the first draft of his famous novel.

The original friary (*convento*)—a small house with a single cleric that served as the base for those enterprising Franciscan missionaries in the sixteenth century—was constructed immediately south of the church, on property that is now the garden of the iconic Casa Braniff. By the end of the nineteenth century the friary was in ruins, used only as stables for the horses owned by the Hotel Arzapalo. It was also the site of lime kilns; the quicklime produced here helped make the plaster and mortar required for building construction.[6] Several early tourist postcards of the town show the heaps of friary rubble that had to be cleared away to build Casa Braniff.

Stagecoach in Calle del Muelle, Chapala, c. 1905. (Anon)

2

Stagecoaches and 1907 traffic congestion

Before the advent of trains or motor vehicles, Guadalajara residents (*Tapatíos*) wishing to visit Chapala had to walk, ride or take a stagecoach (*diligencia*) to the lake. When a Guadalajara-Chapala stagecoach service began in 1866, the trip could be done in ten hours, though it usually took at least twelve.

The situation improved after the Mexican Central Railroad connected Guadalajara to the national railroad network in 1888. The nearest station to the town of Chapala was Atequiza. Most Chapala-bound travelers then went by train to Atequiza where they had the option of either renting a horse or taking the daily stagecoach for the final twenty kilometers to Chapala. The alternative was to take the train as far as Ocotlán and then travel back to Chapala aboard one of the small steamships that offered passenger service.

The stagecoach route from Atequiza followed the *camino real* (Royal road), which passed by the haciendas of Cedros and Buenavista, and skirted the village of Ixtlahuacán de los Membrillos, before climbing over the hills to Santa Cruz de la Soledad on the lake. From Santa Cruz it doubled back to Chapala via the La Labor hacienda.

The excitement of riding the stagecoach was aptly summarized by English author Mrs. Alec Tweedie, who visited Chapala in 1900–1901:

The heavy old coach hanging on thick leather straps swung from side to side; boulders on the road, rivers across the path and suchlike trifles sent us flying from our seats ever and again; but nothing really happened, it was all in the day's work, and nerves are not permitted in Mexico.[1]

The perils of travel and the Mexican Revolution

A century ago, travel, whatever the means, always carried some risks, which included the possibility of running into bandits. English-speaking visitors to Lake Chapala were advised by the 1909 *Terry's Mexico Handbook* that they could expect to encounter many heavily armed individuals—carrying revolvers, rifles or sabres— but that the age had passed of *bandidos*, who formerly "haunted this same highway, stripped unfortunate travellers of every stitch of clothing and usually sent them into Chapala clad in rustling newspapers pinned together with mimosa thorns."[2]

Ironically, Terry's sense of Mexico becoming safer for travelers was proved completely wrong by the outbreak of the Mexican Revolution the following year. By the time the Revolution began in 1910, two newer modes of overland transport—automobiles and motor-buses—were replacing stagecoaches because they were more efficient, safer, and less expensive to operate.

The Hotel Arzapalo owned two stagecoaches for daily service to and from the railroad station, as well as several carriages (*guayines*) for special trips. The daily stage met the train at Atequiza at 1.30pm. The passengers had left Mexico City on the Central Railroad at 9.00pm the previous day and traveled overnight. The stage normally had them in Chapala before 4.00pm.[3]

Service in early years was seasonal, because the summer rainy season damaged or destroyed sections of the route. In 1903, for example, all diligence services were suspended between July and October to enable vital repairs, paid for by the hotel owners, to be carried out to rebuild the road.[4]

Only one small steamboat was based in Chapala in 1899. It was owned by Diego Moreno and made two trips weekly taking passengers and cargo as needed to Tuxcueca, Tizapán el Alto, Cojumatlán, La Palma and Ocotlán. The following year, the Cromptons, a wealthy English family who lived in Chapala, brought a small, Wisconsin-built 30-seat "electrical yacht" named *Carmelita* to the lake. They also had a second, smaller launch named *Carlota*.[5]

The *Carmelita* made regular runs two or three times a week between Chapala, Ocotlán, La Palma and Tuxcueca to support the booming Hotel Arzapalo, with pleasure trips to Mezcala (Presidio) Island on Sundays.

In 1904 the family sold its launches to the Lake Chapala Navigation Company (managed by Julio Lewels) and returned north to Canada.[6]

The *Carmelita* remained in service for several more years, but not without incident. On 18 April 1908 it overturned and its fourteen passengers were thrown into the water. Other boats rushed to their rescue and no lives were lost. The *Carmelita* paid the favor forward two years later by rescuing the passengers of the steamer *Elisa* when her engines broke down near Ocotlán.[7]

Stagecoaches received an unexpected new lease of life during the Mexican Revolution, which began in 1910. While Chapala was spared the worst excesses of violence during the unrest, which lasted until 1920, train services became hazardous and unreliable. Whenever travel by train between Guadalajara and Atequiza was deemed unwise, the stagecoach services from Chapala extended their runs all the way into the big city, following a change of horses or mule teams at Santa Rosa.[8]

In 1920, when Chapala opened its own Railroad Station, it finally became possible to travel all the way to the town by train from Guadalajara, Mexico City or the USA.

Before walking around the town, it is worth standing for a moment outside the Palacio Municipal (Municipal or Town Hall) on the main avenue (Francisco I. Madero) and imagining what the view from here was like in 1907.

Back then, the church was almost entirely out of sight, hidden behind a block of buildings that was demolished in the late 1940s. Only the church spires were visible, rising above a long-established hotel—the Hotel Victor Huber—and a turreted private home. The narrow streets either side of these buildings ended at the lake, and there was no connecting street along the lakefront.

At the end of the street to our right, in 1907, near the pier, the prominent two-story Hotel Arzapalo was doing a roaring trade. It was fully occupied so regularly that its owner, Ignacio Arzapalo, had entrusted a young Guadalajara architect, Guillermo de Alba, to build him a second hotel. This was the Hotel Palmera—the well-proportioned building that the Palacio Municipal occupies today—which was completed in 1907.

Even before the Palmera was built, this street, then known as Calle del Muelle, was often clogged with traffic. Like the Hotel Arzapalo, the Hotel Victor Huber (in the block later demolished) was regularly full. Having two busy hotels facing each other across the street brought temporary chaos whenever their rival stage coaches rumbled into town bringing passengers from Atequiza, the nearest main line railroad station. Turning teams of horses and stage coaches around in the narrow dead-end street must have been quite the sight.

The Hotel Victor Huber, by then renamed the Hotel Gran Chapala, was one of several significant buildings demolished when Avenida Madero was created during the state governorship of Jesús González Gallo (1947–1953). Villa Ana Victoria, one of Chapala's most distinctive early vacation homes, which adjoined the hotel and was separated from the lake by a small formal public garden, was also razed to the ground. Also torn down was a separate structure, built in about 1920 between this garden and the pier, that had become the town's most popular beachfront bar.

Gran Hotel Chapala and Villa Ana Victoria, c. 1930. (Anon)
The Gran Hotel Chapala (left), which had operated as an inn for more than half a century, and the turreted Villa Ana Victoria (right), one of the oldest villas in Chapala, were both demolished when central Chapala was "modernized" to create Avenida Francisco I. Madero at the very end of the 1940s.

3

Gran Hotel Chapala (Posada Doña Trini)

In one guise or another this building operated, first as an inn and then as a hotel, from the 1890s to the 1940s. It was originally known as Posada Doña Trini, named for Trinidad Flores, who owned it with her husband, Francisco.[1] Doña Trini had started her *mesón* in "a three-room shack" close to where the Palacio Municipal is today,[2] before moving across the street in about 1892 to this larger and more solidly-built structure. Doña Trini's is described in various early accounts and was, prior to the opening of the purpose-built Hotel Arzapalo in 1898, the only option for visitors wanting to stay overnight, other than boarding with friends.

In 1903, Posada Doña Trini was rented by an Austrian-born businessman Victor Huber. He re-christened it the Hotel Victor Huber in December that year, before purchasing the hotel for $12,000 cash the following April.[3]

The Hotel Victor Huber prospered, allowing its owner to undertake upgrades every few years. By 1907 it was advertised as the Gran Hotel Victor Huber: a "magnificent hotel, just rebuilt, comfortable, elegant rooms, views of the lake, excellent service, moderate prices. First class bar and restaurant."

Victor Huber had first arrived in Guadalajara in about 1886 as a 20-year-old. Huber imported fine groceries and wines and owned a factory making cigars with tobacco from San Andrés Tuxtla, Veracruz. His company's letterhead, written in English, proudly proclaimed "The Only American Grocery Store in Guadalajara." Huber was well-connected. In 1905, acting on behalf of a wealthy Etzatlán mine owner, he presented the state governor, Miguel Ahumada, with a team of Kentucky thoroughbred carriage horses.[4]

Automobiles and buses

The rise of the automobile made it much easier for wealthy individuals to visit Chapala. One of the the earliest recorded automobile trips from Guadalajara to Chapala was made in April 1906 by Dr. John W. Purnell, a prominent American dentist and long-time resident of Guadalajara. He drove to Chapala in his 8-horsepower Reo in 3 hours 49 minutes.[5] Weeks later, Alfonso Fernández Somellera raced his 30-horsepower Packard the 66-kilometers to the lake in just 63 minutes. Fernández Somellera, in partnership with William Stevens, opened Guadalajara's first car dealership the following year.[6]

Mexico's first ever formal car races, organized by the gentlemen playboys of the Jalisco Automobile Club, were also held in 1907. The original plan, for a race between Guadalajara and Lake Chapala, was abandoned in favor of holding races over a thirty-kilometer course connecting several haciendas near Santa Rosa.[7]

Passenger buses to Chapala started in about 1917 when two Guadalajara business men—Garnot and Maldonat—established a "Wichita" car service between Chapala and Guadalajara. Their converted trucks could carry up to forty passengers, seated five to a bench. The high cost of tickets, frequent breakdowns, rough ride (the vehicles had solid tires) and other inconveniences made the service seasonal and far from ideal.[8] They took three or more hours to reach the lake. Travel time was reduced to about two hours once the road was improved in 1919.[9]

The following year, the La Capilla–Chapala railroad opened, making travel to Chapala simpler, faster and more convenient.

It was not until 1937 that there was an efficient and frequent bus service to Chapala. That year, the newly-formed Cooperativa Autotransportes Guadalajara Chapala y Anexas, S.C.L. (now Autotransportes Guadalajara Chapala, S.A. de C.V.) began offering hourly buses each way from 7.00am to 8.00pm; passengers paid $1.50 (pesos) one-way, $2.50 return.[10]

The Hotel Victor Huber had its own daily stagecoach from Chapala to Atequiza station. The fare for passengers in 1904 was one peso each way.[11] However, when the hotel asked the council for permission to park its stagecoach outside the hotel between trips, it was turned down on the grounds that it would create a precedent for the Arzapalo Hotel to do likewise.

The Hotel Arzapalo and Hotel Victor Huber faced each other across Calle del Muelle and the loading and unloading of stagecoaches in the narrow dead-end street led to many grumbles about traffic congestion. Matters came to a head in 1907 with the completion of a third, even larger, hotel (Hotel Palmera) on the same street. To resolve the problem, the Chapala authorities opened a new street, parallel to the beach, to connect the lakefront end of Calle del Muelle with Calle del Templo. This allowed drivers to proceed along Calle del Muelle almost to the pier before turning left, and then left again, to take Calle del Templo north past the front of the church.

In about 1909 the Gran Hotel Victor Huber, then being managed by Antonio Mólgora, was renamed the Hotel Francés. In 1918 the daily rate was $2.50 pesos a person, including three meals. Mólgora continued to run the Hotel Francés when he also took on the management of the Hotel Palmera—the second hotel owned by Ignacio Arzapalo—in 1919.[12] About four years later Mólgora took over the Hotel Arzapalo.

The Hotel Francés was bought by J. Jesús Cuevas in about 1923 and renamed the Gran Hotel Chapala.[13] By 1925, Cuevas also owned the Hotel Palmera.[14]

The Gran Hotel Chapala was fully occupied over Easter 1923. Its guests at that time included Dr. George Purnell and his daughter, Idella. A few weeks later, D. H. Lawrence and his wife, Frieda, visited Chapala, accompanied by American poet Witter Bynner and his secretary-companion, Willard "Spud" Johnson. Idella had taken one of Bynner's poetry classes at the University of California, so it was natural that the Purnells quickly became good friends with these illustrious literary visitors. The Gran Hotel Chapala was still in operation almost two decades later when Bynner, who lived in Santa Fe, New Mexico, returned to Chapala and bought a house near the plaza as his second home.

Villa Ana Victoria, c. 1905. (Anon)

4

Villa Ana Victoria

Villa Ana Victoria, one of Chapala's most distinctive buildings on early photographs, was built facing the lake in the 1890s by Prussian émigré Eduard Collignon and named for his wife, Ana Victoria Stephenson. Separating it from the beach was a small fenced garden, laid out in a formal manner on land belonging to the municipality. Immediately behind the house was the Posada Doña Trini, accessed from Calle del Muelle.

Villa Ana Victoria was built prior to 1896 and, according to some accounts, was one of several homes built in Chapala by Septimus Crowe.[1] However, Crowe's early houses were usually wooden cottages whereas this villa, sturdily built of stone, looked more like a town house. Regardless of architect, the turret on the villa's southwest corner makes it instantly recognizable on early images of the town center.

Tragically, Ana Victoria died suddenly on 5 April 1897, not long after the Chapala house was completed. *The Mexican Herald* reported that "Mrs. Edward Collignon, wife of the wealthy banker and merchant, died after illness of but two hours on Monday." She was interred in Guadalajara's "new cemetery", the same one where the remains of Juan Jaacks, a German landowner murdered in Ajijic, had been the inaugural burial six months earlier. Ana Victoria's interment was attended by a large circle of her friends, "many of whom sent cut flowers which, contrary to local custom, were placed upon her grave."[2]

Following her untimely passing, the family scarcely visited the house during the following year. By December 1898, when Eduard Collignon was reported to be remodeling the house, his brother, Theodor (Teodoro), had also built a vacation home in Chapala,[3] for his own wife (Amalia Esqueda) and their numerous young children.

The municipality decided in 1907 to solve the stagecoach congestion outside the hotels by opening a new street, running parallel to the beach, connecting the lakefront ends of Calle del Muelle and Calle del Templo. This required using most of Eduard Collignon's "private" garden, as well as part of an adjoining formal public garden known as El Jardín del Muelle. Eduard complied with the council's request to move his fence back so that the new road could be completed.[4]

The Sánchez beachfront bar, c. 1925. (Anon)

5

The Widow's Bar

In 1920, José Edmundo Sánchez—with the support of his architect friend Guillermo de Alba—started Pavilion Monterrey, a bar where food and drinks were served in an open-air pavilion facing the lake.[1] The bar was in a prime location, only meters from the beach, between the Hotel Arzapalo (the Beer Garden today) and the Braniff mansion (Cazadores restaurant).

Coincidentally, both Sánchez and de Alba were expert photographers; their discerning eye and considerable talent have given us many sensitive and artistic images of Chapala, among the finest images of the town ever taken. Sánchez was keen to profit from his skills; photos of the exterior of the bar show an advertisement in massive letters proclaiming that picture postcards can be purchased inside.

José Sánchez's wife, María Guadalupe Nuño, helped run the bar, perhaps to make sure her husband and his pals did not drink all the profits. A few years after the bar opened, she offered her husband a shot glass of home-made chaser—freshly-squeezed orange juice, spiced up with salt and powdered red chile peppers—to accompany his favorite tequila.

This chaser proved so popular with the regular patrons that they soon demanded their own "sangrita" ("little blood") with their tequilas. The concoction's intense red color, from which it derived its name, was later intensified by adding vegetable coloring. This was the origin of sangrita, whose fame quickly spread nationwide.

In 1926, when de Alba left Chapala for Mexico City, Sánchez and his wife were left to run the bar on their own. All went well for a number of years until tragedy struck in July 1933 when Sánchez, then aged 45, died at home from a gunshot wound.[2] María continued to manage the

Lioness on the prowl

At about the same time as Sánchez died, a specially-commissioned plinth was placed alongside the bar for a unique twenty-year-old sculpture. The sculpture, of a lioness, had been created by master stonemason Faustino Gil from Cocula, who helped build the twin towers of the parish church.[3]

The medium for Gil's sculpture was volcanic ash collected from the streets of Chapala after the major eruption of Colima Volcano in January 1913.[4] A clothing store owner, Nicolás Barragán, offered local youngsters two cents for every box of ashes collected, and commissioned Gil to make the lioness. Originally placed outside his store, the statue was later moved to the Post Office (then on Avenida del Muelle) and then to its plinth by the Widow's Bar, where it held pride of place on the Chapala beachfront.[5]

Later photos show only an empty plinth. When Avenida Francisco I. Madero was created, the plinth was destroyed. The precise whereabouts of the lioness are unknown; perhaps she is still wandering the streets at night....

bar, which became known as the Cantina de la Viuda Sánchez (Widow Sánchez's bar).

The untimely loss of her husband did not slow María's efforts to popularize sangrita. She continued to offer it to her customers, who took to calling the spicy mixture "Sangrita Viuda de Sánchez", a name which stuck. Over the years, with tasting sessions no doubt enjoyed by all, the recipe for sangrita was perfected by adding small amounts of other fruit juices and some hot sauce to provide more bite.

María—Widow Sánchez—gained such renown that she found her way into more than one book about Chapala. Arthur Davison Ficke praised her as a "very famous cook" in his one and only novel, *Mrs. Morton of Mexico,* published in 1939.[6] Two years later, Mary Frances Kennedy Fisher, a celebrity cook and prominent cookery writer, visited Chapala for several weeks to stay with her brother David and his wife, Sarah, who were honeymooning at the lake. Afterwards, Fisher recalled her visit to the Sánchez restaurant-bar:

> There was a bar on the lake, under a kind of roof. It was too expensive for the village people, but enough tourists and weekenders from Guadalajara came to keep fine silk dresses and heavy bracelets on the fat

widow who ran it. She was a white-faced woman with a sly, flashing smile, and welcomed me warmly. I ordered the kind of cocktail the children told me they always drank there, and I could see her smiling toward a prosperous future as she stirred the liquors.[7]

In 1946, Canadian author Ross Parmenter spent a few days in Chapala and visited The Widow's Cantina, "an open pavilion where visitors and tourists gathered to drink and chat." A meticulous observer, Parmenter loved the view over the lake and the bar's relaxed ambiance:

And the air was filled with music. The patrons of the widow's establishment were perpetually serenaded by bands of strolling mariachis. The particular group playing for us consisted of three violinists, a trumpeter, a ukulele player and two guitarists, one of whom had an instrument with a very deep sound box. The squeaking fiddles and the throbbing guitars consorted strangely together, and the penetrating tootling of the cornet made the instrumental family still more incongruous. Yet the resulting music had an odd sort of charm. And every now and then the men sang in high tenor voices. I could not understand the words and some of the music was undoubtedly sad. But again, even in the expression of the sadness, I had the sense of listening to people bidding me take life easy.[8]

By the time the restaurant was demolished to allow for the creation of Avenida Madero and Paseo Ramón Corona, Widow Sánchez was making far more profit from her sangrita than from the restaurant-bar. Her children began the large-scale commercial production of sangrita in 1950 and later developed and marketed Cholula Hot Sauce, named for the 2500-year-old city in central Mexico. The family sold the rights to their original brand names—"Sangrita de la Viuda de Sánchez" and "Cholula Hot Sauce"—some years ago, but Widow Sánchez's great-grandchildren continue to commercialize new versions of sangrita and hot sauces under the "Lago de Chapala" label. Their factory is the town's largest manufacturing plant.

Orange juice remains the principal ingredient of sangrita. Although oranges are not native to Mexico, their use in Chapala is especially fitting. The Lake Chapala area was famous as long ago as the sixteenth century for producing both oranges and orange blossom, used for wedding bouquets, cooking, candies, teas and perfumes.

Columbus brought the first oranges to the Americas on his second voyage (1493–96). In 1586, less than thirty years after Sebastián de Párraga planted the first orange trees in the friary at Chapala, a visiting chronicler remarked that Chapala had so many fruit trees that:

> the entire village is like an orchard. The Indians make a lot of orange blossom water and from it a lot of money. It is so fertile for oranges that, in the garden of the friary where there are many of these trees, they took from a sweet orange tree a branch that had eleven good, big, mature, yellow oranges, crammed together on top of each other.[9]

Casa Barragán, 2016.

6

Casa Barragán (the Witter Bynner house)

On the east side of Avenida Madero at number 411, a few buildings up the street from the church, is Casa Barragán—a white, two-story modernist house in dire need of conservation.

This had belonged to the Barragán family, who owned a hacienda in the hills on the south side of the lake, since the end of the nineteenth century. The family used the house as a staging point on their trips to and from Guadalajara. One of their offspring, Luis Barragán (1902–1988), Mexico's most famous architect, ably assisted by colleague Juan Palomar y Arias, subsequently transformed this home in 1931–32.[1] Eight years later, the house was bought as a vacation home by the American poet Witter Bynner, who had first visited Chapala in the company of D.H. Lawrence in 1923. *Journey with Genius*, Bynner's memoir of this trip and the group's time in Chapala, is engagingly-written and crammed full of recollections, fun stories and anecdotes.

After purchasing their second home, Bynner and his companion, Robert "Bob" Hunt, who lived most of the time in Santa Fe, New Mexico, became regular visitors to Chapala. Bynner spent two and a half years in Chapala during the second world war and the equivalent of ten years of his life in the town in total.

Their mutual friend, artist John Liggett Meigs, described how Hunt had added "an extensive rooftop terrace which had clear views of Lake Chapala and nearby mountains" to the house, located a short distance from the lake and very close to the town's plaza.[2]

Bynner was a controversial figure in the American poetry world. He had collaborated with Arthur Davison Ficke in 1916, for example, to perpetuate an extended prank aimed at deflating the self-important poetry

Luis Barragán Morfín

Luis Barragán Morfín (1902–1988), the most influential Mexican architect of the twentieth century, was raised in Guadalajara and graduated as an engineer from the Escuela Libre de Ingenieros in 1923. During an extensive trip to Europe and Morocco, Barragán heard lectures by Le Corbusier and became familiar with the ideas and work of Ferdinand Bac. Inspired by their modernist approach, he returned to Guadalajara in 1926 and worked alongside his brother, Juan José, before establishing his own architectural practice.

Barragán designed a number of homes in Guadalajara and Chapala between 1930 and 1936, before moving to Mexico City to develop the residential area of Jardines del Pedregal. His house and studio, completed in 1948, are now listed as a UNESCO World Heritage site. Barragán was also responsible, with partners, for Torres de Satélite (1957) and the residential areas of Las Arboledas and Lomas Verdes, all in the proximity of Ciudad Satélite in the state of México.

Barragán had a solo exhibition at the Museum of Modern Art in New York City (1976) and is the only Mexican ever to have won the prestigious Pritzker Architecture Prize (1980).

In Chapala, Barragán remodeled the home belonging to his family on Francisco I. Madero, and undertook several commissions, including construction or renovations of the "D. H. Lawrence" house on Zaragoza, Villa Robles León on Paseo Ramón Corona, and Villa Adriana and Jardín del Mago, both on Hidalgo. He also designed a bandstand, long since demolished, for the central plaza.[3]

Following his death in 1988, Barragán's ashes were interred in the Rotunda de los Jaliscienses ilustres in Guadalajara. In a macabre twist, some of his ashes were later turned into a diamond ring by American conceptual artist Jill Magid. Magid's 2019 documentary, *The Proposal*, details her bizarre attempt to exchange the ring for the Barragán archives, currently in private hands in Switzerland, and repatriate them to Mexico.

commentators of the time. Their joint creation of a fictitious female poet, whose work was subsequently published to rave reviews in august poetry journals, was one of the great literary hoaxes of the twentieth century.

Bynner loved Chapala: "The Mind clears at Chapala. Questions answer themselves. Tasks become easy." He was quick to acknowledge in the 1950s how much the town had changed since he first got to know it:

> The "beach" where Lawrence used to sit, is now a severe boulevard [Ramón Corona] which gives me a pang when I remember the simple

village we lived in. The tree under which he sat and wrote is gone long since and the beach close to it where fishermen cast nets and women washed clothes has receded a quarter of a mile. But the mountains still surround what is left of the lake and, as a village somewhat inland, Chapala would still have charmed us had we come upon it in its present state."[4]

Witter Bynner was one of the most prolific composers of poems related to Lake Chapala (and Mexico) of all time, and included a number of these poems in his collection *Indian Earth* (1929), which many critics view as his finest work, and which he dedicated to Lawrence. One reviewer wrote that,

> Chapala, a sequence occupying over half the seventy-seven pages of the book, is a poignant revelation to one in quest of the essence of an alien spirit, that alien spirit being in this case the simple, passionate Indian soul of old Mexico.[5]

According to some sources, Bynner lent his Chapala home in the summer of 1945 to the then almost unknown playwright Tennessee Williams. During his short stay at Lake Chapala, Williams penned the first draft of *A Street Car Named Desire*.

Bynner's long-time partner, Robert Hunt, died in 1964. The following year Bynner suffered a serious stroke. He sold his Chapala house, complete with all its contents, soon afterwards to Meigs and another well-known artist, Peter Hurd.

Meigs was particularly taken with the fact that the house had once belonged to Barragán, whose architectural work had been an inspiration for his own architectural designs. Meigs and Hurd did not own the house for long. Much as they liked the property initially, they lost heart when they discovered that the owners of a nearby two-story hotel (presumably the Palmera/Nido) had spoiled the view of the lake from their rooftop terrace by selling the airspace on the hotel roof for a massive twenty foot by forty foot billboard proclaiming "Brandy Presidente."[6]

Shortly before selling, Hurd rented the house out in 1968 to another prominent American artist, Everett Gee Jackson. Jackson had lived in Chapala for a couple of years in the mid-1920s, allegedly renting Lawrence's former residence immediately after the great English author departed Mexico for New York.

After a period of time being used as warehouse space for a local supermarket, this valuable historic building is in desperate need of some tender, loving care. It would make a wonderful space for cultural events and exhibitions.

The old plaza, Chapala, c. 1905. (Photo by José María Lupercio; pub: Al Libro de Caja, Guadalajara)

7

Plazas, old and new

At the northern end of the long since demolished block that contained Villa Ana Victoria and Posada Doña Trini was a small plaza or *jardín*. Located approximately where the fountain in the center divide of Avenida Madero splashes today, this central plaza (Jardín Juárez) was especially lively during civic and religious celebrations. For instance, one observer in 1898 described how,

> With the Día de la Purísima [8 December], Chapala has awakened from its customary sloth and is now a blaze of lights mixed with the odor of a very inferior grade of powder. All the Indians from the surrounding towns are crowding its plaza and the chewed up bits of sugar cane make walking somewhat difficult.[1]

In an effort to improve decorum, the town council announced in 1910 that it was no longer allowed for anyone to walk onto the plaza wearing a straw sombrero (the type used by local *campesinos*).[2]

Walking north along Madero, pause for a moment at the stop lights. The cross street to the left is Avenida Hidalgo, formerly Calle del Agua Caliente; to the right is Morelos, formerly Calle del Horizonte.

The building at the northwest corner of this intersection was Chapala's first Palacio Municipal. One section of this lovely old building, which was inaugurated in 1910, is now a downtown cultural center. Shortly after the building opened, a second *jardín* was created in front of it, giving Chapala twin central plazas either side of the east-west street. Both these plazas were replaced when the current plaza—with its bandstand—was created a short distance away during the extensive remodeling of the center of Chapala at the end of the 1940s.

The street that defines the northern side of the plaza is López Cotilla, originally known as Calle de San Miguel. To the west, this street dead-ends on the lower slopes of Cerro San Miguel, which rises steeply above the center of Chapala.

The site of the current plaza had previously been shared by a market and the General Eugenio Zúñiga school. The school, which had been inaugurated in about 1938, was relocated to Calle Niños Heroes, and the market was replaced by the two-story covered market that is still in use today.

This market, which was formally opened on 31 October 1951, is named for José Encarnación Rosas, a local-born hero of the War of Independence. Encarnación Rosas was a leader of the rag-tag band of insurgents, several hundred strong, who took refuge on Mezcala Island in 1812 and successfully repelled all attempts by the mightier and better equipped Royalist troops and navy to dislodge them. The four-year stand-off ended in 1816 with an honorable truce, and the insurgents were allowed to return to their lakeside villages without further reprisals.[3]

At the start of the twentieth century Chapala's market would have been an open air *tianguis*. Very few photos of Chapala are known that depict village people going about their everyday lives at this time, and one early postcard—despite being titled "Chapala Market"—actually depicts the open-air market in the distant village of El Salto, a village nearer to Guadalajara than Chapala! Published and sold by Juan Kaiser of Guadalajara, this particular card is a timeless scene showing prospective purchasers inspecting the fresh produce displayed by market vendors on the sidewalk; clearly the titles of cards like this one were designed to appeal to the broadest possible audience.

The genuine Chapala market was described in 1910 by the Polish traveler Vitold de Szyszlo, who was making his way through Mexico and was enthralled by what he saw when he stayed at Chapala:

> The market, in the center of the village, is the meeting point of all these colorful people. Under multicolored awnings are mounted pyramids of fruit and vegetables, bananas, oranges, lemons, watermelons, melons, papayas, *mameyes*, lettuces, sweet potatoes, red and hot peppers. Elsewhere, zealous merchants offer fresh tortillas and tamales of golden cooked corn, and pulque, the smell of which fills one with intense repulsion. On the other side of the square, cluttered stalls display sombreros, wool sarapes and leather huaraches.[4]

Casa Verde

Typical of the wanton architectural destruction that has plagued Lakeside towns in recent decades is the loss of Casa Verde (Green House). Until a few years ago, this significant and historic building stood immediately behind the present-day market, at the southeast corner of the intersection of Calle Juárez with Calle López Cotilla. After the edifice was allowed to fall into disrepair, it was demolished, even as arguments raged about its cultural value and restoration potential.[5]

The original property, in 1906, was a small house built by Miguel Cuevas. The next owners—Ambrosio Ulloa and his wife, Lorenza Martínez Negrete—purchased the house in 1918 and remodeled it over the next decade into a much more substantial dwelling. After earth movements resulted in some structural damage, the Chapala Public Works Department requested permission from federal authorities in 2001 to demolish part of the building. They were still awaiting a response when a section of the building's facade fell into the street, fortunately without causing any injuries or other serious consequences. Notwithstanding those who protested, the building was completely torn down a few years later.

Cerro San Miguel, undated. (B. de Alba)
This view is looking west along Calle de San Miguel (now López Cotilla).

View from Cerro San Miguel, c. 1953. (J. González)
Taken shortly after the completion of Avenida Francisco I. Madero and Paseo
Ramón Corona, this photo reveals the massive area of dusty former lakebed that
was exposed during the severe drought of the mid-1950s.

8

Cerro San Miguel

Overlooking the market and center of Chapala is the small volcanic hill known as Cerro San Miguel (Saint Michael's Hill). In early colonial times this was the site of one of the two hermitages in Chapala, in each of which a resident lay brother lived, largely dependent on local people for fresh produce and food.[1] The other hermitage was on Mezcala Island.

When young American author Charles Embree and his wife, Virginia, spent an extended eight-month honeymoon in Chapala in 1898, they rented "a white stone cottage on the river road under the shadow of Mt. San Miguel."[2] Embree was working on his first novel, *A Dream of a Throne, the Story of a Mexican Revolt,* the first novel in any language to be set entirely at Lake Chapala.[3] The opening scene is a fisherman's hut at nightfall, by which hour "the shadows of St. Michael's hill, which rises high and rocky out of the town's center, had long since fallen across the Chapala plaza."

Embree's novel displays an accurate and astute knowledge of the area's nineteenth century history and of the various villages on both shores of the lake; details of clothing, beliefs, customs, events and habits all ring true. The novel is a romance story which examines the conflicts between Indians and Spaniards, identical themes to those later explored by D. H. Lawrence in *The Plumed Serpent*, the first draft of which was written only a few streets away in 1923.

During Embree's time, Cerro San Miguel was owned by the municipality of Chapala. When officials decided in 1908 that Chapala needed funds to build its first Palacio Municipal, they sold the hill for $25,000 to three men from Guadalajara—Antonio Pérez Verdía, Manuel Aldrete and José Prieto—who planned a new attraction for the lake resort:

That portion overlooking the lake will be terraced, and the terraces divided into lots for cottages. A cog railroad for the accommodation of those having cottages on the mountain enters into the plans.[4]

Work was expected to begin within a year. However, as was true for many other grandiose plans of the time, they were abandoned at the start of the Mexican Revolution.

Over the years, Cerro San Miguel has been climbed by numerous photographers in search of the perfect vantage point from which to capture the best view over the town and the lake to the mountains beyond.

In the 1930s, Basulto Limón asked Guillermo de Alba to design a walkway to the top of Cerro San Miguel with shelters and pergolas near the top to serve the needs of visitors who climbed the hill for the panoramic view. [5] Sadly, this plan was apparently never carried out.

Former Town Hall, Chapala, February 2020.

9

Old Municipal Building

Work on building the old Palacio Municipal (at the intersection of Avenida Madero and Avenida Hidalgo) began in 1908, when Manuel Capetillo Villaseñor was the *presidente municipal*. Chapala was growing rapidly and it was Capetillo who orchestrated the sale of Cerro San Miguel to finance the construction of the town's first council offices.

A stately two-story building (architect unknown) with a fine facade was erected at the intersection of Avenida Madero and Avenida Hidalgo and was formally acquired by the town in 1910, shortly after Capetillo left office. The building was remodeled in 1940.

Chapala received city status in 1970. A decade later, local authorities bought a privately-built, architecturally-congruent adjoining wing to boost their administrative space.[1] The old building had served area residents well for almost a century before parts of it were declared unstable, due (ironically, given how the building was funded) to the frequent earth movements on the lower slopes of Cerro San Miguel. Minor faults and tremors have, over the years, damaged many other buildings in the vicinity.

Given the safety concerns, the municipal administration of Alberto Alcántar (1998–2000) was forced to relocate all government offices. After a few years in far-from-ideal temporary locations, the city purchased the former Hotel Nido as its new headquarters in 2001, a building of similar age and beauty to the original.

Refurbishment of the original town hall (Antiguo Palacio) began in 2007 and it reopened as a cultural center, with 214-seat auditorium and exhibit spaces, in 2015.

Hotel Palmera, Chapala, c. 1908. (Calpini)

10

Municipal Building (Hotel Palmera, Hotel Nido)

Walking back towards the pier, stop for a moment by the current City Hall (Palacio Municipal). Dating back to 1907, this was originally the Hotel Palmera, which first opened for business the following year.

The Palmera (named for a single tall palm tree in its central courtyard) was the brainchild of Ignacio Arzapalo, whose existing eponymous hotel, opened almost a decade earlier, was regularly full to overflowing. Indeed, within months of the opening of the Hotel Arzapalo, the rising popularity of Chapala meant rooms were already at a premium, especially during Easter week and major holidays.

As early as summer 1900, the need for another modern hotel had been noted by the *El Paso Times*:

> The hotel accommodations have been taxed to the utmost in Chapala for the past three months and at the present time many persons are sleeping in tents and boats. It has been necessary to secure rooms for months ahead, and to pay "exposition" rates. All this has convinced some local and some other capitalists a large hotel run on the American plan, with several employees speaking English, is a necessity.[1]

Confident of success, Arzapalo commissioned Guillermo de Alba to build him a new hotel, with instructions to make it larger and even better appointed than the hotel he already owned. When construction of the 60-room hotel, built at a cost of $100,000, was completed in 1907, Arzapalo offered the building for rent, describing it as a "modern construction, brick, iron and cement", with "American furnishings, electric bells" and a "dining room for 400 people." It also had a staggering $7000-worth of fine woodwork, supplied by the Chihuahua Lumber Company.[2]

When the Hotel Palmera formally opened in 1908, its first manager was Francisco Mantice, who had previously been at the Hotel Arzapalo. The Palmera was fully-booked even though the rooms had still not been painted![3]

An inveterate Italian traveler, Adolfo Dollero, who visited Chapala in 1907-08, was suitably impressed:

> We were staying in the Hotel Palmera, belonging to a congenial Italian citizen Mr. Francisco Mantice. The hotel was first rate and the cooking, distinctly French and Italian, was therefore very satisfying.[4]

Later managers of the Hotel Palmera included Antonio Mólgora, manager of the Hotel Francés, who ran both hotels simultaneously for a time before he moved to the Hotel Arzapalo in late 1923 or shortly thereafter. In the mid-1920s, the Palmera was acquired by J. Jesús Cuevas.[5] The building was subsequently divided into two independent hotels. The northern wing, bought by Luis Cuevas (J. Jesús Cuevas's nephew), became the Hotel Niza, which survived into the 1940s. The southern wing was purchased by Spanish-born Ramón Nido, who had been in Mexico for more than twenty years, and his Mexican wife, Sara, who had previously owned a cantina in Guadalajara.[6] They reopened 29 guest rooms of the former Palmera in 1930 as the Hotel Nido.[7]

Gran Hotel Nido luggage label.

Claims that the famous Mexican actress María Félix and her first husband, Enrique Álvarez, spent the first night of their honeymoon at the hotel the following year may be plausible in terms of timing but do not match what the movie star wrote in her autobiography: "We spent our honeymoon in a hotel in Atotonilco el Alto... that was a chamber of torture to me... it took two weeks for Enrique to take my virginity."[8]

After the hotel's architect, Guillermo de Alba, left for Mexico City in 1926, his wife and daughter, Mina, moved to the Hotel Nido. In February 1933, Mina left from here to travel the short distance to her civil marriage ceremony aboard a boat on Lake Chapala before returning to shore for the religious ceremony in the parish church. The newly weds spent their honeymoon at Villa Josefina, owned by Nettie Schnaider a family friend.[9]

After Ramón Nido's death in 1945, Roberto Cuevas (another nephew of J. Jesús Cuevas) rented the building. With the assistance of other family members, he ran the hotel for more than forty years. When Sara Fregoso de Nido, who had inherited the building from her husband, died in 1962, it was sold to Luis Cuevas Pimienta (Roberto's brother) and his wife Natalia Gómez, who respected the stipulation that the hotel's name never be changed.[10]

The Nido established itself as a premier hotel and was favorably reviewed for its inexpensive hospitality in every guide book for several decades. A 1941 review, for example, promised that, "Out at Chapala the Hotel Nido, freshly painted in white and lettuce green, gives you room and bath and a lake view for a pittance."[11]

The Cuevas family ran the Hotel Nido successfully until 1994. Seven years later, the beautiful, Guillermo de Alba-designed building was repurposed as the town's Palacio Municipal. Step inside, if it is open, to admire the magnificent 240-square-meter mural depicting local history, painted by energetic Ajijic artist Efrén González in the building's stairwell.

Hotel Arzapalo, c. 1907. (Photo by José María Lupercio? Pub: Manuel Hernández)

11

Hotel Arzapalo

The earliest iconic building in Chapala that is still standing (aside from the church) is immediately south of the former Hotel Palmera and was originally the Hotel Arzapalo. Fronting onto the beach, this was a magnificent two-story building when it opened its doors for the first time in 1898. Today, a line of small stores occupies what remains of the side of the building, with the Beer Garden restaurant-bar making use of part of the front of the former hotel.

The Hotel Arzapalo was a truly remarkable project. Not only was it the area's earliest purpose-built hotel and the first substantial purpose-built hotel in any small community anywhere in Mexico, but it was financed entirely by domestic (Mexican) capital and not by foreign investment.

Though the design of the hotel is commonly attributed to architect Guillermo de Alba, it seems inconceivable—to me at least—that de Alba was commissioned for the design, though he may have helped with the building's construction.[1] Groundbreaking for the hotel was in 1896, barely a year after de Alba had graduated as an engineer-surveyor at the age of 21.[2] Moreover, de Alba's name does not feature in any of the contemporary accounts of the construction or opening of the hotel.

When the correspondent for *The Mexican Herald* spoke with "Don Guillermo de Alva" [sic], shortly after the Hotel Arzapalo opened in 1898, he described him as "a young gentleman of Guadalajara, now here and engaged with Mr. Henriquez in house construction."[3] This strongly suggests that de Alba had only recently moved to Chapala, and gives no hint that he might have already undertaken any ambitious hotel project right at the start of his career. Additionally, it stretches credulity to believe that a prominent successful businessman like Ignacio Arzapalo would

Ignacio Arzapalo Palacios

Ignacio Arzapalo Palacios (1837–1909), the man behind the Hotel Arzapalo, was born in the mining town of Cosala, Sinaloa, in 1837 and died in Guadalajara on 6 May 1909 at the age of 72.[4]

Arzapalo was living in Guadalajara in February 1877 when he took 16-year-old María Pacheco as his second wife in a ceremony at the Sagrario Metropolitano.[5] Their son, José Ignacio Arzapalo Pacheco, was born in the city the following year.

In partnership with several other prominent investors, Arzapalo formed a company in 1881 to build a Guadalajara-Tlaquepaque railroad.[6] Despite their best efforts, this project proved unsuccessful.

A few months before Arzapalo was elected to the Guadalajara city council in 1888,[7] his wife's diamond necklace was used to test the skills of visiting American mentalist Washington Irving Bishop. The necklace was hidden, without the mystic's knowledge, a mile away from the Hotel Humboldt (now Hotel Francés) where he was staying. Wearing a blindfold, Bishop was placed in a carriage and proceeded to give such precise instructions to the driver that he was taken directly to the necklace—to the cheers and applause of thousands of onlookers.[8]

As well as opening his eponymous hotel in Chapala, Arzapalo was a co-founder in 1902 of the Jalisco Development Company, and of the first Chapala Yacht Club in 1904.

Though these projects were not immediately realized, they were a clear sign that Chapala was about to be transformed into one of Mexico's most desirable vacation destinations. Arzapalo's many contributions to Chapala were crucial steps in transforming a small fishing village into Mexico's premier lakeside resort.

entrust a project of this magnitude to a completely unknown 22-year-old architect when there were other, larger, more experienced firms (such as George King and his associates) readily available in Guadalajara. Proving the identity of the Hotel Arzapalo's architect may be impossible, but King must be one of the more likely contenders.

The visionary investor behind the Hotel Arzapalo was Ignacio Arzapalo Palacios, a native of Sinaloa, who had multiple business interests in Guadalajara.

Why did Arzapalo build a hotel in Chapala? A contemporary account asserts that, when the wealthy businessman had fallen ill a few years earlier, his doctors suggested he take the most famous water cures in Europe. When these failed to achieve the desired result, Arzapalo returned to

Guadalajara and tried the baths at Chapala, following which he was "soon restored to perfect health."[9] Coincidence or not, the timing of Arzapalo's cure closely matches the first occasion when the virtues of Chapala's medicinal waters were extolled internationally—at a medical conference in Philadelphia.[10]

The promenade that protected the front of the Hotel Arzapalo was first created in 1891 when Ignacio Arzapalo was given permission to widen a platform he had already built on the lakeshore side of his property. A few years later, Arzapalo began constructing his two-story, 36-room hotel.[11] The Hotel Arzapalo opened in March 1898 with a "superb banquet" attended by state governor Luis Curiel, General Carballeda (the commander of the Fifth Zone), British consul Lionel Carden, Septimus Crowe and many others.[12]

Rates at the new hotel were between $2.50 and $4.00 a day, depending on the room, more than twice the then daily rate across the street at the Posada Doña Trini.[13]

Advertisements for the hotel extolled the virtues of the climate, the rooms, the location and the town's medicinal waters, as well as the hotel's own "pleasure boats and baths on the lake."[14] Other advertisements called Lake Chapala "The Switzerland of America" and boasted that the Hotel Arzapalo was "The only inland Bathing Resort in the Republic."[15]

The Hotel Arzapalo's first manager was Italian-born Alberto Anzino, who absconded the following January with more than 1000 pesos in gold, silver and bank notes.[16] This valuable booty was recovered when Anzino was arrested in Durango a few days later. Despite his bad luck with Anzino, Arzapalo clearly liked having the hotel managed by an Italian. At least three more early managers of the hotel—Francisco Mantice, Francisco Olivero and Antonio Seimandi—were also Italian.

Arzapalo and his second wife, María Pacheco, had a single child: José Ignacio Arzapalo Pacheco, born in 1878. José Ignacio Jr. married Aurora Pérez Verdía (daughter of lawyer Luis Pérez Verdía) in 1900, and their only child—María Aurora—was born the following year. Tragically, her mother died shortly after giving birth and, after also losing her father in 1904,[17] María Aurora was raised by her paternal grandparents.

When Ignacio Arzapalo Sr. died in 1909, only a year after the formal opening of Hotel Palmera, his elegant second hotel, it was his grand-daughter, María Aurora (not yet eight), who inherited both hotels (worth an estimated $350,000) plus life insurance and property in

Hotel Arzapalo (left) and former Hotel Palmera (right), February 2020.

central Guadalajara (worth $250,000). Even if these numbers are pesos, this inheritance was worth US$300,000 at the time, equivalent to $7.5 million today. Land records show that ownership of the Hotel Arzapalo was transferred to María Pacheco, his widow, in 1911.

Arzapalo's will appointed Lic. Enrique Pazos to be María Aurora's guardian and manage her affairs until she came of age,[18] an arrangement immediately challenged by Luis Pérez Verdía, her maternal grandfather. The ever-impatient Pérez Verdía then decided to take matters into his own hands. He kidnapped the girl in broad daylight from a public park in Guadalajara and successfully contested both Pazos' right to be her guardian and to administer her share of the estate.[19] This sequence of events led to sensationalist headlines and articles in the press.[20]

According to one version, headlined "Wealthy Orphan Vanishes,"

"Aurora Arzapalo... [an] orphan and heiress to millions has been kidnapped and can not be located anywhere. The police have arrested several suspects among the relatives all of whom are wealthy but would fall heir to some of the Arzapalo millions if the child were out of the way."[21]

To complicate matters further, Pérez Verdía died in 1914, at which point María Aurora, still barely a teenager, returned to live in Chapala with her paternal grandmother, María Pacheco.

By that time the unrest of the Revolution had caused investors, especially those close to President Díaz, to either flee or keep an extremely low profile. Visitor numbers to Chapala plummeted, hotels struggled and, as sporadic fighting continued, there was little hope of recovery. For several years, most Chapala hotels, if they opened at all, did so only seasonally; the number of tourists did not justify them remaining open year-round.

Things picked up in 1919 when the Gran Hotel Arzapalo took display ads to inform readers that it had been recently renovated and offered French cuisine, special suites for couples, and fair prices.[22] The road between Guadalajara and Chapala was improved, reducing travel time (in theory) to about two hours each way. Sunday trips from Guadalajara by "rapid and comfortable bus with pneumatic tires" were advertised. The bus left Guadalajara at 8.00am and departed Chapala at 5.00pm; tickets were $4.00 pesos each way.[23]

The following year the Chapala Railroad Station finally opened. It enabled visitors to travel all the way to Guadalajara or Mexico City via train (with one or two transfers), heralding a new period of optimism as regards tourism.

The Hotel Arzapalo remained a popular hotel into the 1920s. In May 1923, for example, when D. H. Lawrence and his wife, Frieda, rented a house nearby, their traveling companions—poet Witter Bynner and Willard "Spud" Johnson—stayed at the Hotel Arzapalo for more than two months.

Under the management of Antonio Mólgora, who had previously managed the Hotel Francés and the Hotel Palmera, the Hotel Arzapalo was temporarily rebranded as the Hotel Mólgora from about 1924 to 1927. When severe summer rainstorms in 1926 swelled the lake to its highest level for decades, downtown Chapala was flooded; the water rose well above the elevated sidewalk in front of the Arzapalo hotel and lapped against several private homes. For a time, the lake even covered the pier.[24] The railroad tracks and station were also inundated and rail services to Guadalajara had to be suspended.

After Mólgora's death in 1927 the hotel went back to its old name. The building was bought from María Pacheco in 1941 by Guadalajara storekeeper Bohumil Hubička, and the hotel remained in business for most of the 1940s, becoming especially well known for its restaurant and live music. Nacho Pérez and his jazz band were a regular and popular attraction at the hotel for many years.

The Hotel Arzapalo was purchased in 1949 by state politician Jesús González Gallo, the Governor of Jalisco from 1947 to 1953. González Gallo hoped to refurbish the building in keeping with the suggestions made by one of his sons, Federico, an architect who had written a thesis about how the site could return to glory as a luxury hotel with a swimming pool on its upper floor. These plans were never realized. As of 2019, the property remains in the González Gallo family, with plans for the hotel's restoration still pending.

The building has been extensively modified over the years. The east side of the hotel originally had seven windows in its upper story, and six in the lower story, with a doorway below the window furthest from the beach. The northernmost section (with doorway below a window) was demolished, leaving only six windows on the upper floor. At the same time, several of the ground floor windows have been converted into narrow doorways, such as that used to access the Oxxo minimarket.

The Beer Garden, c. 1960. (J. González)

12

Beer Garden

Part of the lakefront section of the former Hotel Arzapalo was subsequently incorporated into the Beer Garden restaurant-bar.

Chapala was so popular in the early 1930s that many column-inches in local papers were devoted to the names of Easter week visitors from Guadalajara (and further afield) vacationing in the town. This captive market led to Monterrey-based brewery Cervecería Cuauhtémoc establishing a lakefront Beer Garden in April 1933; it was constructed in a matter of days.[1] The Beer-Garden Cuauhtémoc, built next to the Arzapalo Hotel, opened on 13 April, with Ramón Nido supplying the bar and restaurant service.

This may not have been the first Beer Garden in Chapala. I have been unable to substantiate Natalia Cuevas's version that a Beer Garden was started in 1926 by her father-in-law, Luis Cuevas Sr.,[2] with the encouragement of a former classmate, Javier García de Quevedo, who worked for Cervecería Cuauhtémoc.

Natalia Cuevas and her husband, Luis Cuevas Jr., began managing the Beer Garden in December 1940 and soon turned it into a veritable institution, widely acknowledged as the preferred place to meet friends, sip beer and while away an afternoon to the sound of Mike Laure[3] and competing mariachi bands. From Mexican presidents, state governors, famous movie stars, foreign celebrities and local residents to Tapatíos enjoying a day at the lake—they all loved the Beer Garden.[4]

The latest iteration of the Beer Garden (in a slightly different location to the original) opened on 30 July 2008, occupying, in part, what was originally the "Salón Mirador" of the ground floor of the Arzapalo Hotel.

Few patrons of the Beer Garden over the years have probably ever realized that they are downing their cervezas and shots of tequila almost exactly on the site of a small Franciscan chapel and Hospital de los Indios (Hospital de la Inmaculada Concepción) which served the local community centuries ago, or where a small glass factory, utilizing the silica-rich sand from the beach, operated in the nineteenth century.[5]

The lakefront restaurants immediately west of the Beer Garden occupy property that was once used for the area's earliest lawn tennis courts. They were laid out in 1918, just after the end of the first world war, by Guillermo de Alba, commissioned by Ramón Castañeda y Castañeda, whose daughter, Margarita, had learned to play tennis "while at one of the best schools in England" and was one of the top players in Guadalajara.[6]

Casa Capetillo, c. 1900. (Ignacio Arzapalo)

13

Casa Capetillo

A short distance along the promenade from the Beer Garden, on the eastern corner with Aquiles Serdán (Porfirio Díaz) is Casa Capetillo (Aquiles Serdán 25). Though its exact age is unknown, it was certainly one of the earliest "cottages" in Chapala, and was an obvious landmark on the Chapala shoreline from the early 1890s.[1]

Despite its common attribution to Manuel Capetillo Villaseñor (1878–1932), who served as *presidente municipal* of Chapala from 1905-1909 inclusive, the land documents for this property prove it belonged to his father, Manuel Capetillo Quevedo (1848–1922), owner of Hacienda Buenavista near Ixtlahuacán de los Membrillos.

One possible reason for the misattribution is confusion arising from the official list of municipal presidents of Chapala which names Manuel Capetillo Villaseñor as becoming *presidente municipal* for the first time in 1898 (when he would have been only 20 years of age) and later serving successive terms from 1905–1909 inclusive. It is far more likely that the *presidente municipal* in 1898 was his father, Manuel Capetillo Quevedo.

That Manuel Capetillo Sr. owned the house in Chapala is supported by a paragraph in *The Mexican Herald* in 1898 reporting that "Manuel Capetillo, Jefe Politico of this district, has returned to Chapala and is now, with his family, occupying his villa on the shores of the lake."[2] That was the year Manuel Capetillo Sr. turned fifty. His first wife, Josefa Villaseñor Calderón had died three years earlier (after giving him at least seven children, including Manuel Capetillo Jr.), and he had taken Refugio Dávalos as his second wife. At the time of the newspaper piece, Manuel Capetillo Jr. had not yet married or started a family; he wed 21-year-old María del Rosario González in La Barca fourteen years later.

Following Manuel Capetillo Sr.'s death in 1922, the property passed in equal parts to four of his children: Manuel Jr., Guadalupe, María Elena (wife of the Norwegian railroad engineer Birger Winsnes), and Guillermo. Not long after, the house was rented out to members of the Collignon family.

The girl who died from eating mangoes (1926)

According to Natalia Cuevas, the house later belonged to "Eduardo Collignon who was married with Amparo Godivar" (sic), and the couple had three children: Eduardo, Mario and Ana Victoria, the youngest. Cuevas recalled how, as a child in the 1920s, she used to play with her friends in the mango orchard behind their home. The kids liked to eat the mangoes before they were ripe. It was eating these green mangoes, said Cuevas, that caused the death of Ana Victoria, "the only daughter they had," from a severe case of typhoid.[3]

This particular account is an especially interesting example of how reconstructing historical accounts long after the event from personal recollections is fraught with difficulty. The land records prove that the house never belonged to anyone in the Collignon family, though one generation of the family seems to have occupied it during the 1920s. However, this was not the "Eduardo Collignon who was married with Amparo Godivar," but his father (Eduardo Collignon Stephenson), the son of Eduard Collignon and Ana Victoria Stephenson, the owners of Villa Ana Victoria. Cuevas has inadvertently mixed up two different generations of the same family.

Eduardo Collignon Stephenson (1886–1957) married María de la Peña Arias in 1914; they had four children, two boys and two girls. This is the family that occupied Casa Capetillo in the 1920s. One of their daughters, Guillermina, died as an infant in 1918, before the time Cuevas is writing about. Tragically, their other daughter, named Ana Elena (not Ana Victoria), also died young, of typhoid at the tender age of 10 on 6 August 1926. Her death certificate confirms that this tragic event occurred at "Casa Capetillo."

It was one of Ana Elena's brothers, Eduardo Collignon y de la Peña (c. 1915–1977), who later (1944) married Amparo Luisa Goribar (not Godivar as in Cuevas' account) Díaz González (1924–1977).

Cuevas concluded her account by describing how the body of the young girl was taken by special train to Guadalajara during a frightful storm, and how the family never returned to Chapala. Indeed, so much rain fell that summer that the lake rose to what would prove to be its highest ever level during the twentieth century; the Chapala–La Capilla railroad, which connected with the main line to Guadalajara, ceased to operate a few months later.

The year after their tragic loss, Eduardo Collignon Stephenson and his wife traveled with their two sons to Germany for an extended visit, where they left their elder son Eduardo to complete his formal schooling.[4]

The four Capetillo Villaseñor siblings who owned the property sold it to Carlos Camarena in 1931. He sold it on the following year to Luz Orendain Gutiérrez de González Luna, the wife of Guadalajara lawyer Víctor González Luna. They expanded the property into an imposing multilevel mansion. In the 1980s their son—Víctor González Luna Orendain, also a lawyer—romanced the Hollywood star Elizabeth Taylor. Following their engagement in August 1983, the great American actress visited the former Casa Capetillo several times to spend time with the wealthy young lawyer she so nearly took as her eighth husband.

Barbara Ann and Richard Lee Henderson acquired the house in 1998 and then carried out extensive renovations. When the historic home was placed on the market again in 2018, it was listed as having two *casitas*, a Moroccan folly, covered terraces, romantic gardens and several fountains, while the interior boasted many original features, such as stained glass windows, domes, high wood-beamed ceilings, and a "musicians' balcony in the main reception room (repurposed as a cozy library)." The views of Lake Chapala from its upper stories were described as incomparable.[5]

Standing in front of Casa Capetillo today, it is hard to believe that it, and the entire block just described (including the Hotel Palmera and Hotel Arzapalo), narrowly escaped demolition in the 1930s. An unnamed foreigner proposed that both this block, and the next one to the east (with the Gran Hotel Chapala and Villa Ana Victoria) be expropriated and replaced with a large plaza and a luxury 5-story hotel with swimming pool and tennis courts. Fortunately, wiser heads prevailed—at least on this occasion—and this "absurd and ill-intentioned" proposal was totally rejected.[6]

Casa Galván, c. 1907. (Photo by José María Lupercio. Pub: Manuel Hernández)

14

Casa Galván (Villa Aurora)

The next waterfront building (Paseo Ramón Corona 23) is the Lake Chapala Inn, an imposing structure that grew out of an early house known first as Casa Galván and then Villa Aurora. Its most notable occupant, historically, was Norwegian entrepreneur Christian Schjetnan, the visionary early promoter of Chapala who was eventually successful in completing the branch railroad to the town from the Mexican Central mainline at La Capilla.

Casa Galván was built at the start of the twentieth century. In 1904, a contemporary newspaper listed it as one of several homes "under construction or recently completed."[1] It reportedly cost its owner, Mrs. Gabriela Galván, about $12,000, significantly less than the $40,000 spent by Luis Pérez Verdía to build his home (later Casa Braniff) or the $20,000 Carlos Navarro Mora invested in his "cottage."

Gabriela Galván was the daughter of General Pedro A. Galván and his wife, Gabriela del Río. In 1885, at the age of 21, she married a young lawyer, Rafael Dionicio Saldaña Bravo, in the city of Puebla. The couple's daughter—Gabriela Saldaña Galván (1888–1970)—was born in Guadalajara and spent much of her childhood in Chapala. During a regatta there in 1908, she rowed alongside María Guadalupe Capetillo Villaseñor (one of Manuel Capetillo, Jr.'s sisters) in a pairs rowing race that was watched by President Díaz and other dignitaries.[2]

The earliest land records for Villa Galván show that Gabriela Galván was already widowed when she acquired the property in two separate transactions in 1900, buying land first from Mauricio Delgadillo and then from María Fermina Enciso. Galván began construction of her house almost immediately and retained ownership until she sold it to

Paul Christian Schjetnan

Paul Christian Schjetnan (1870–1945) was born in Kristiansund, a port town on the west coast of Norway, and arrived in Mexico City in 1898, apparently acting on behalf of the Norwegian government.[3] Given his prominence in Norwegian-Mexican circles, and his later ties to Lake Chapala, Schjetnan undoubtedly knew Septimus Crowe, the Norwegian-born, yacht-loving, former British vice-consul to Norway, who had frequented Chapala from the late 1880s.

In 1901, Schjetnan founded the Norwegian-Mexican Company, whose main line of business was importing telephones from Norway.[4] The company also won a potentially very lucrative fishing concession in Veracruz for the rights to all fishing (including oysters, lobster and shrimp) for a period of 15 years.[5] This concession was later revoked.

It is unclear when Christian Schjetnan and his wife, Leonor Dantan, first lived in Chapala. A few months after the couple married in 1908, Schjetnan nearly died from typhus;[6] perhaps, like so many others before them, they decided that Lake Chapala was the best place for him to recuperate.

Schjetnan quickly saw the untapped potential of the Chapala region. In partnership with others, Schjetnan promoted projects to build a new recreational island in the lake (which never got started), export local agricultural products to the USA (a proposal that floundered), and to fire up tourism by building a yacht club, railroad and hotel. The yacht club was completed in 1911 and the railroad in 1920; sadly, neither lasted very long.

Schjetnan never lost his idealism. In 1932, for example, he wrote to *The New York Times* calling for the establishment of a worldwide Universal Peace Association—or "Pax Mundi"—to promote disarmament and avoid "a new world war where millions of people would be slaughtered and billions of dollars squandered."[7]

Schjetnan was one of the most visionary individuals ever to live at Lake Chapala and, unlike most "blue sky" thinkers past or present, he had the drive and ability to achieve many of his goals. His legacy lives on.

María Pacheco (the widow of Ignacio Arzapalo) in April 1916.[8] It was presumably María Pacheco who renamed the house Villa Aurora, in honor of one or both of the two Auroras in her life: her late daughter-in-law and her only grand-daughter, orphaned as a child.

The land documents revealed one major surprise: the absence of any mention of Christian Schjetnan. It turns out that the often-cash-strapped

Schjetnan never owned Villa Aurora, but only rented it for the many years he and his family lived in Chapala. Even so, it may well be Schjetnan who was responsible for remodeling it into a much larger and grander house.

In 1934, at about the time the Schjetnans left Chapala and returned to Mexico City, María Pacheco sold the property to Tomás Orozco Sainz and Elisa Velasco de Orozco.

Villa Aurora was later owned by several members of the extensive Castellanos family, before eventually being given a new lease of life as the Lake Chapala Inn, owned and operated by Alicia Segura de McNiff.

Mi Pullman, 2019.

15

Mi Pullman

Aquiles Serdán, the narrow street between Villa Capetillo and Casa Galván, was originally named Porfirio Díaz and was created in 1899 on land bought from Manuel Capetillo for $50.[1] A few meters up this street (the shortest in Chapala) are two noteworthy properties: Mi Pullman and Villa Ave María.

Mi Pullman, on the west side of Aquiles Serdán at number 28, a mere stone's throw from Schjetnan's Villa Aurora, was architect Guillermo de Alba's family home. De Alba worked closely with Schjetnan and was entrusted by him to design the Chapala Railroad Station, which opened in 1920.

Built on an unusually narrow lot, Mi Pullman is one of the most distinctive private residences in Chapala. De Alba had visited Chicago before returning to Chapala in about 1896 to start a construction business. When he decided to build his own family home, he opted for a tall, skinny building modeled after a Pullman rail car. The house was completed in 1906 and the house-warming party for the completed residence was a grand formally-attired affair, as was to be expected given de Alba's growing reputation as an architect.

A couple of years before de Alba moved to Mexico City in 1926, he sold the property to Salvador Ugarte. It changed hands again in 1933, when Beatriz Rollieri de Camarena purchased it, and yet again three years later when it was acquired by Modesto Barreto.[2] By the 1990s, and many transactions later, the building had fallen into a terrible state of repair, despite rooms on the ground floor being used as the local tourism office.

Fortuitously, a visiting Englishwoman, Rosalind Chenery, fell in love with the dilapidated building, then inhabited only by swallows and bats,

Guillermo de Alba

Guillermo de Alba (1874–1935)[3] was born in Mexico City. His family moved to Guadalajara in 1885, where he attended the Escuela Libre de Ingenieros and graduated as an Ingeniero Topógrafo (engineer-surveyor) in 1895.[4]

De Alba apparently then spent some time in Chicago where he was influenced by the Chicago School (a style or movement, not an institution). During his time in Chicago, de Alba likely studied numerous recently-completed buildings and perhaps met Dankmar Adler and Louis H. Sullivan ("form follows function"), who had dissolved their own architectural partnership a year or two earlier in 1894.

In his early twenties, de Alba returned to live in Chapala and worked in construction with Manuel Henríquez.[5] Over the next two decades he designed and built numerous fine residences and commercial buildings. In Guadalajara these included the Hotel Fenix, Casa Abanicos and Villa Guillermina.

In 1906, de Alba was working for the Guadalajara city council when he was entrusted with the major project to divert the Río San Juan, which flowed through the center of the city, into a tunnel so that Colonia Moderna could be created. The project involved two other engineers with close ties to Chapala: Carlos Ochoa Arroniz (Villa Ochoa) was responsible for leveling the ground and making the streets, while Rafael de la Mora (Villa Carmen) was given the task of installing the water supply and drainage systems.[6]

That same year, de Alba built his own family home—Mi Pullman (1906)—in Chapala, before completing the Hotel Palmera (1907), Villa Niza (c. 1919), and the Chapala Railroad Station (1920).

When fund raising began in 1916 to build a new automobile road between Guadalajara and Chapala, de Alba was elected the group's treasurer. Several prominent individuals each gave $5000 to supplement the state government grant of $23,300.[7]

Besides his work as an architect, de Alba was also an excellent photographer. We are indebted to him for some of the finest pictures of Chapala during the early years of the twentieth century. We are also indebted to de Alba for the earliest street plan of Chapala, dating from 1915.

De Alba married Maclovia de Cañedo y González de Hermosillo (1859-1933) in Chapala in 1900; their only child, Guillermina, was born two years later.

After moving to Mexico City in 1926, de Alba worked as a draftsman in the Secretaría de Recursos Hidráulicos drawing designs for bridges and dams.[8] After Maclovia's death, he married Cristina Villamil, with whom he had another daughter.[8]

in 2004 and decided to buy it. She spent the next four years locating the multiple owners and persuading them to sell.

Only after finally acquiring the property did she discover that, while the land taxes were up-to-date, no taxes had ever been paid on the building itself! After rectifying this minor detail, Chenery set about renovating this Art Nouveau townhouse to its former glory, inside and out.[9] The building still has many of its original fixtures and fittings, including oak wood parquet flooring, stained glass windows, tile floors and a cast iron bath tub. The views from the top of this tastefully and sympathetically restored home are magnificent, encompassing the pier, lake and distant mountains on the far side of the lake.

Villa Ave María, 1919. (Guillermo de Alba)

16

Villa Ave María

The property known as Villa Ave María, more or less opposite Mi Pullman, on the other side of Aquiles Serdán at number 27, is a few years older than Mi Pullman and dates back to the end of the nineteenth century. The architect of the original residence (since remodeled beyond recognition) is unknown.

The earliest title records for the property show that Mrs. María Guadalupe Capetillo (daughter of Manuel Capetillo Sr., owner of Casa Capetillo, and sister of Manuel Capetillo Jr.) bought part of it in 1916[1] and later combined it with adjoining land she inherited from her husband, Alfonso Martínez, as his sole heir after he died in 1919. This may be when Guillermo de Alba remodeled the property into the stately villa he photographed.

According to land tax records, María Guadalupe Capetillo owned four residences in Chapala in 1924, all acquired between 1915–1920. Their combined value for tax purposes had been reassessed that year and had risen from $3466 pesos to $9500. The assessed value of Villa Ave María rose from $1500 to $5000, suggesting it had been significantly enlarged or upgraded since its previous valuation. Her other three houses were on Juárez, Pesquería (Zaragoza today) and Calvario (Guerrero).

María Guadalupe Capetillo sold Villa Ave María in 1933 to Vicente Saborio, who transferred it two years later to a corporation, "La Equitativa, Compañía Mexicana de Urbanización, S.A." It then passed through a series of hands before being acquired in 2006 by Barbara Ann Henderson and Martha Gibson Rogers. This beautiful building was registered in 2010 as a multifamily condominium with three units sharing common areas.

* • ● • *

Villa Paz, 2009.

17

Chalet Paulsen (Villa Paz)

Returning to the waterfront, a short distance further west is Villa 1927 Arthotel Boutique. This superbly-restored building was originally known as Chalet Paulsen and later as Villa Paz. The formal address of this property, which extends back to the highway, is Hidalgo 234.

Chalet Paulsen was built in around 1900 as the vacation home of the Paulsen family of Guadalajara.[1] The patriarch of the family was Ernesto Paulsen, a wealthy German-born businessman who moved to Guadalajara as a 20-year-old in 1879 and later owned La Palma, Guadalajara's most prestigious furniture and hardware store. Paulsen was the honorary vice-consul in Guadalajara for Sweden and Norway.[2]

When President Porfirio Díaz visited Guadalajara to open the railroad to Ameca in 1896, Paulsen took personal charge of decorating the patio of the University of Guadalajara for the most extravagant party Guadalajara had ever seen.[3] The patio was turned into a massive ballroom with 50 huge mirrors and drapes made from dozens of rolls of fine crepe and gauze to give the kind of over-the-top opulence more associated with a European court than a provincial and traditional Mexican city. No expense was spared: the centerpiece of the decorations was a massive 200-lamp chandelier. The evening was a huge success, with 3000 invited guests enjoying dinner, music and dancing.

Díaz attended the party as guest of honor but it was nearly his last. Two days later, after a formal banquet on Mezcala Island in the middle of the lake, he came close to losing his life when the boats carrying him and his party back to shore, and the safety of the presidential train waiting for them in Ocotlán, struggled to say afloat during a ferocious storm on Lake Chapala.[4]

Charles Lincoln Strange

Charles Lincoln Strange (c. 1865–1908) was an American architect active in Guadalajara in the first decade of the twentieth century.

Born in Ohio, Strange had previously been the superintendent of buildings for the city of Los Angeles. In Los Angeles, Strange is credited with designing or co-designing Orange County Courthouse No 1 in Santa Ana, the Hotel Green in Pasadena, the Central Police Station at First and Hill, and numerous city schools.[5]

Strange left Los Angeles in 1900, following the breakdown of his first marriage,[6] and moved to Guadalajara, where he designed the Banco de Londres y México and built, in 1906, the Hotel San Francis (Hotel Imperial).

Strange may have been the architect of Chalet Paulsen. He became a close personal friend of Ernesto Paulsen and the two men worked together on a proposed hotel for Isla de los Alacranes in 1904. Later that year, Strange also drew up plans for the first Chapala Yacht Club.

Strange and his partner, María Isabel García, had two children in Guadalajara and married in May 1908, just as Strange's heart problems forced the family to leave Mexico for California. When Strange departed from Guadalajara, he left all his property and business affairs in Paulsen's hands. After Strange's death a few weeks later, Paulsen took charge of settling his estate.[7]

The original architect of Chalet Paulsen, with its distinctive roofline, is unknown, but may have been Charles Strange, an American architect then working in Guadalajara, who was a close personal friend of Paulsen.

Paulsen had numerous business interests besides his hardware store. At the start of the twentieth century, he even owned the Isla de los Alacranes (Scorpion Island) for a few years, hoping to turn it into a recreational center and sporting resort.[8]

Paulsen also held a majority stake in the Lake Chapala Navigation Company, which was actively involved in supplying a steamship service on Lake Chapala in the first decade of the twentieth century.[9] Along with other prominent Guadalajara businessmen, Paulsen also formed the Jalisco Development Company. Based in Guadalajara, with agencies in Mexico City, New York and London, this company planned an electric railroad linking Guadalajara to Chapala. Its ambitions extended to bringing electricity to the north shore villages, including Jocotepec and Chapala, building large-scale irrigation works, and installing a public water system to supply residents with potable water. Finally, it intended to build a serviceable road to Guadalajara.[10]

The company succeeded in getting electricity installed, at least in Chapala, but failed completely in its efforts to establish a municipal potable water system. As for the road, it was several decades before driving from Guadalajara to Chapala was commonplace, and several more before it was easy. As recently as the 1970s, foreign residents regularly referred to one section of the Chapala–Ajijic road as the Ho Chi Minh Trail.

When life insurance was introduced in Mexico, Paulsen was at its forefront. He took out policies for himself (payable to his company) and for his wife (payable to her family), insuring his own life for a total of $475,000, making him the most heavily insured man in the city at the time.[11]

Following Paulsen's death in 1916, Chalet Paulsen passed to German Blank, one of his sons-in-law, who had married Paulsen's stepdaughter, Elisa Neimann Paulsen (1881–1919),[12] and was a partner in Paulsen's furniture business, La Palma.

Blank sold the property almost immediately to Ignacio E. Castellanos (c. 1870–1938) and his wife, Paz González Rivas, after whom the villa was renamed.[13] Castellanos came from a family with immense historic association with Lake Chapala. In the nineteenth century, his parents— Ignacio E. Castellanos and poet Esther Tapia de Castellanos—farmed an immense spread of prime agricultural land near Ocotlán, centered on the Hacienda San Andrés, and whose domain included the resort area later known as the Rivera Castellanos.

Ignacio Castellanos Jr.'s older brother, Luis, was (albeit briefly) mayor of Guadalajara (1916–1917) and Governor of Jalisco (1919–1920); he was also the father of renowned architect Pedro Castellanos Lambley, who designed Villa Ferrara.

Paz González Rivas became the outright owner of Villa Paz in 1936. After her death, the property was bought in 1948 by her sister, Pilar González Rivas de Arce. It remained in the Arce family for more than half a century, slowly falling into disrepair.

Local names for Villa Paz over the years have included Casa de los Mangos (for the numerous mango trees that formerly shaded the house) and Casa del Eiffel, on account of its use of steel beams, a supposed connection to architect Gustave Eiffel. Sadly, Eiffel had already retired from his architectural practice by the time Casa Paulsen was built and is not known to have designed any private residences.

Fortunately for the heritage of Chapala, the sadly dilapidated Villa Paz was given a new lease of life in 2012, after it was acquired by Stephanie and John Decker. It took them three years (2014–2017) to restore this magnificent property into a boutique hotel, Villa 1927 Arthotel. In a nod to the rich architectural history of Chapala, its twelve suites are named after important local buildings.

18

Las Delicias therapeutic baths

Immediately west of Villa Paz (and best seen from the lakeside promenade) the palapa-covered El Quetzal events space and swimming pool is the site of Chapala's first public thermal-water baths, known as Las Delicias.

The therapeutic qualities of the waters of Chapala had been remarked upon, perhaps even enjoyed firsthand, for centuries. Father Antonio Tello, for instance, writing in about 1650, described how, "This village has a pool of most excellent hot water, which emerges and flows from a very attractive small hill close by. Emerging from the foot of the hill are springs which, collected in tanks made of stones and lime, form two pools."[1]

After American journalist George Wythe Baylor visited the medicinal baths in Chapala in 1902, he explained that "The baths are of both iron and sulphur water and just warm enough to be pleasant." He described "a cement tank, some four feet wide and deep and six feet long," as well as one that was "more of a swimming pool, some 12 feet wide, five or six feet deep and 40 or 50 feet long." He reported that the price to use them was 15 cents if you were supplied with soap and towels, and 10 cents if you brought your own."[2]

When President Díaz visited Chapala a few years later to stay with his wife's inlaws, he took a daily bath in the health-giving "Las Delicias" pools each morning.[3]

It is believed to be these pools, open to the public for many years, where, in 1941, young Californian artist David Holbrook Kennedy (1919–1942) painted the area's earliest known murals. Sadly, both the building and murals have long since been destroyed. Soon after arriving at Lake Chapala, David had married his American girlfriend, Sarah, in Ajijic.[4] Their ceremony, on 11 October 1941, was one of the earliest all-American marriages in the area, and one of the area's first destination weddings.

The murals, finished in November 1941, required several weeks of arduous work. David was assisted by his new bride and two of his sisters, one of whom—foodwriter Mary Frances Kennedy Fisher—later described how they had "spent several hours every day neckdeep in the clear running water of the pools, walking cautiously on the sandy bottoms with pieplates full of tempera held up, and paintbrushes stuck in our hair."[5]

The Las Delicias pools closed in the 1950s when an earthquake diverted the flow of water away from its original course and caused the springs supplying the pools to dry up. At that time, Roberto Cuevas was managing the pools and their adjoining restaurant. Cuevas subsequently founded the Balneario San Juan Cosalá.

Today, many other locations in Chapala, including Villa Montecarlo, a private club and hotel with extensive gardens sloping down to the lake, still offer the same pleasantly warm, therapeutic mineral water that helped put Chapala on the map more than a hundred years ago. All this thermal water, incidentally, is one of the on-going beneficial vestiges of the area's ancient volcanic history, and also helps explain the presence of silver and gold ores in the hills along the lake's northern shore.

Villa Ferrara, c. 1950. (J. González)

Part B

19

Villa Ferrara

The residence immediately west of where the *malecón* (promenade) meets Avenida Hidalgo is Villa Ferrara (Hidalgo 240A), one of the more imposing villas on mid-century photos of the shoreline.

The current Villa Ferrara, which dates back to about 1935, was the work of architect Pedro Castellanos Lambley, one of several distinguished Mexican architects who designed and built the period homes in Chapala that now give the town its architecturally eclectic appeal. Castellanos also designed Villa Adriana, a short distance further west.

The commission to design Villa Ferrara, presumed to be named after Ferrara in Italy, came from Tequila Cuervo heiress Lupe Gallardo González Rubio (1897–1964).[1] She inherited the company (the best-selling tequila brand in the world) in 1934 from her aunt, Anita González Rubio y de la Torre, whose husband was a direct descendant of the founder.[2] Not long after receiving her inheritance, Lupe, who managed the company until 1957, asked the firm of Castellanos y Negrete (Enrique Martínez Negrete) to design her the perfect vacation home.

Villa Ferrara, exemplifying Mexican modernism, is one of the crown jewels of the so-called Guadalajara School of Architecture (Escuela Tapatía de Arquitectura). This elegant residence was photographed at about the time of its completion by American photographer-architect Esther Baum Born, who was documenting the rise of Mexican modernist architecture.[3] The house and grounds boast a variety of spaces designed to shield occupants from the outside world while offering ever-changing plays of light and shadow. This villa, like many other buildings in the vicinity, originally utilized the local thermal spring water as its source of hot water.

Pedro Castellanos Lambley

Modernist architect Pedro Castellanos Lambley (1902–1961) was raised in a high society Guadalajara family that excelled in literature and politics. His grandmother was the poet Esther Tapia de Castellanos.[4] His father was Luis Castellanos Tapia, governor of the state of Jalisco 1919–1920, and his mother was Carolina Lambley Magaña. One of his uncles—Ignacio Castellanos Tapia—purchased Villa Paz in Chapala (jointly with his wife) in 1918.

Castellanos studied in the UK and the USA prior to entering the Escuela Libre de Ingenieros in Guadalajara. After graduating as an engineer in 1924, Castellanos worked with Luis Barragán's brother—Juan José Barragán, a prominent builder—before partnering with Enrique Martínez Negrete y Palomar (1901–1968) to start an architectural practice. Castellanos y Negrete quickly gained an enviable reputation for appealing and successful designs representative of early modernism.

Castellanos designed several stately family homes in Guadalajara, as well as the city's San Juan de Dios market (which was replaced in the 1950s). In Chapala, his masterpiece was Villa Ferrara, though he also had a hand in several other modernist residences.

In the 1930s, Castellanos and a fellow architect, Juan Palomar y Arias, proposed an ambitious plan, never realized, called (ironically) "El Plan Loco" ("The Mad Plan") for a utopian, visionary and futuristic Guadalajara. This involved creating a 120-meter-wide ring of circulation around the city and a series of districts, divided by broad boulevards and linear parks and walkways linking to a massive green central park space—a genuinely ecological city.[5]

Castellanos was one of Guadalajara's most successful and highly respected architects by 1938, when he became a Franciscan priest. From then on, he focused almost exclusively on designing ecclesiastical buildings, such as the chapel at Ciudad Granja, the Templo de Nuestra Señora del Sagrado Rosario in Guadalajara, and the tower and entrance to the church of San Miguel Arcángel in La Manzanilla de la Paz, south of Lake Chapala.

The walls and ceiling of the main dining room of Villa Ferrara are decorated with a fine mural, showing indigenous people fishing and working the land, painted in 1950 by Michoacán-born artist José María de Servín,[6] whose work also adorns the Chapala Yacht Club.

Later owners of Villa Ferrara included Manuel Aguilar Figueroa, a former co-owner of El Manglar. In the early 2000s, Villa Ferrara was acquired by Lorenzo Landeros Ochoa and his wife, Silvia Volquarts. They undertook much-needed restorative work, such as replacing the drainage system, electrical wiring and some of the floors, thereby ensuring that Villa Ferrara, which retains many of its original fixtures, should serve its occupants well for many more years.

Villa Ferrara occupies only the easternmost portion of what was originally a single, large, 30,000-square-meter plot of land owned in the late-nineteenth century by Manuel Cuevas, the town's *presidente municipal* in 1897.[7] Cuevas sold the entire property in about 1894 to Englishman Lionel Carden, who built Villa Tlalocan. Twenty years later, the property was subdivided and three additional villas were built: Villa Ferrara and Villa San José to the east of Villa Tlalocan, and Villa Adriana (also designed by Castellanos) to its west.

Chapala bottling plant label, undated.

20

Mineral water bottling plant

Almost opposite the former Villa San José, at the foot of Cerro de San Miguel, on the north side of the street at Hidalgo 243,[1] was the thermal Sánchez spring, site of the mineral water bottling operation of Salvador Pérez Arce in the first decades of the twentieth century. The spring was named for a former owner, Marcos Sánchez, and its calcium carbonate content was considered ideal for strengthening bones and neutralizing any excess stomach acid.

According to an early advertisement, placed in December 1907 for the warm water's curative properties, the Sánchez spring originated from a depth of about 400 meters and the water emerged from the ground at a temperature of 35 degrees Celsius.[2]

A few months earlier, Salvador Pérez Arce, after acquiring the spring from Sánchez,[3] had asked the municipal authorities for permission to install a small kiosk in the town plaza, outside the market, to sell flavored drinks and potable water from this spring to the public.[4]

In partnership with his only son, also named Salvador, Pérez Arce installed a bottling machine and began marketing ferruginous mineral water using the somewhat unimaginative brand name "Chapala."[5] They later enlisted the help of José María Schnaider (who owned La Perla brewery in Guadalajara and a vacation home, Villa Josefina, in Chapala) to seek export markets.[6]

The flavors in the "Chapala" line of beverages included sparkling water, lemonade (which masked the slightly metallic taste of the mineral water), ginger, and orange, an experimental flavor that was short-lived. In addition, they sold El Cerrito de San Miguel purified water by the demijohn (*garrafón*).[7]

When Pérez Arce died in 1915, his son (a cousin of Chapala architect Guillermo de Alba) assumed control. The bottling business was subsequently inherited by one of his sons, Gabriel.[8]

Despite their best efforts, the local bottling operations eventually lost out to the much larger-scale nationwide brands, such as Tehuacán (from the eponymous town in the state of Puebla) and imported foreign colas.

Villa Tlalocan, c. 1945. (J. González)

21

Villa Tlalocan

At Hidalgo 244, Villa Tlalocan, completed in 1896, originally occupied the entire 30,000-square-meter property owned by Manuel Cuevas. Lionel (later Sir Lionel) Carden, the British consul in Mexico, bought the land in about 1894 and commissioned a stately vacation home for himself and his New York-born wife, Anne Eliza Lefferts.

Carden (1851–1915) first visited Mexico in the early 1880s. After serving a short stint as British vice-consul at Havana in Cuba (where the British consul-general at the time was Arthur de Capel Crowe, a half-brother of Septimus Crowe), Carden was appointed British consul at Savannah, Georgia. From Savannah, he was sent to Mexico City to ascertain how best to develop British trade in Mexico, how to manage the Mexican bonds held in England, and what steps were needed for the renewal of diplomatic relations between the UK and Mexico. Following Carden's report, a preliminary agreement to renew relations was signed on 6 August 1884.

This re-opened Mexico for British investors and it is no coincidence that another well-connected British diplomat, Septimus Crowe, moved to Mexico at this time. Crowe knew Carden both professionally and personally; they had various acquaintances in common. It is entirely possible that it was Crowe who persuaded Carden, after the latter was formally confirmed as the consul general of Great Britain in Mexico in 1886,[1] to build his vacation home in Chapala.

Carden's duties as consul inevitably required him to spend most of his time in Mexico City. However, his wife much preferred Chapala to Mexico City; as soon as their grand holiday home was finished in 1896, she lived almost full-time at the lake.

George Edward King

George Edward King (1852–1912) was a progressive British architect who had moved first to the US and then to Mexico. He practiced in the US for about twenty years, and designed a number of grand buildings there, including Old Main at Colorado Agricultural college (now Colorado State University) in Fort Collins; the Tabor opera house, post office and hotel, all in Leadville, Colorado; the Presidio county court house in Marfa, Texas; and the Wells Fargo Express offices in El Paso, Texas. Many of these buildings still stand.[2]

In the 1890s, King set up shop in Mexico City, with a local partner, as King y Ochoa. The company established offices in several cities, including Guadalajara, Durango and Chihuahua. In 1908, King managed the Guadalajara office personally, while leaving his son, Arthur, in charge of the Mexico City office.[3] The firm undertook numerous major commissions. It designed the former customs house (now Museo Histórico) in Ciudad Juárez, theaters in Zacatecas, Durango and Chihuahua, and remodeled Palacio Mayor, the main post office in Mexico City, as well as the Government Palace and Degollado Theater in Guadalajara.[4]

In Chapala, King was responsible for Villa Tlalocan and Casa Braniff, and may have had a hand in other buildings of the period.

When the Revolution began in 1910, King and his family fled to Texas, where both George and his wife, Harriet, died two years later.

To design their Chapala home, Carden commissioned noted British architect George Edward King, who had offices in several cities in Mexico, including the capital. King brought one of his associates, Charles Grove Johnson, from New York to Mexico City in 1895 to personally direct

> construction of the very beautiful chalet that Mr. Lionel Carden plans to erect on the shores of Lake Chapala. It will be modern, beautiful and cost about $10,000 dollars.[5]

Taking inflation into account, that amount equates to $300,000 today. The construction of Villa Tlalocan took almost a year to complete.

Villa Tlalocan was not King's only work in Chapala. He was later asked by Guadalajara lawyer and historian Luis Pérez Verdía to build the so-called Braniff mansion, now the Cazadores restaurant. Given their apparent architectural similarities with Casa Braniff, King (or perhaps Johnson) may also have played some part in designing Villa Reynera and Villa Virginia, two other turn-of-the-century residences in Chapala.

Once Villa Tlalocan was completed, in April 1896, Carden and his wife shipped all the necessary furnishings from Mexico City by rail to Ocotlán. For the final leg of the trip, everything was transferred to a small boat (*canoa*), to be towed by the steamship *Chapala* to their new home. Near Mezcala Island, stray sparks from the ship's funnel set fire to a mattress in the *canoa*.[6] The fire spread so rapidly that the *canoa* (ironically named La Providencia) had to be cut loose; it sank to the bottom of the lake, taking all the Cardens' furnishings with it. Keeping his resolve with an archetypal British stiff upper lip, Carden ordered replacements which arrived that summer. And, only a few months later, in December 1896 the Cardens were ready to entertain President Díaz and "two or three of his party" for breakfast at Villa Tlalocan, immediately prior to the sumptuous state banquet being given in Díaz's honor on Mezcala Island.[7]

The following year, the Cardens hosted the President's wife, Carmen Romero Rubio, at Villa Tlalocan over Easter.[8] A contemporary account described the Carden estate:

> In the midst of a large garden and lawn stands the spacious, substantial and hospitable house of Mr. Carden. The bath-house with its boats and gaily-striped awnings makes a pretty spot of color. A small army of workmen must have been employed to build this house so quickly, to say nothing of a mountain having been partly demolished to form the foundations.[9]

Following a visit in 1898, another journalist wrote that the Cardens' two-story house was:

> the largest, costliest and most complete in Chapala... a happy minglement of the Swiss chalet, the Southern verandahed house of a prosperous planter and withal having an Italian suggestion. It is tastefully planned and is set amid grounds cultivated and adorned with flowers so easily grown in this paradisiacal climate where Frost touches not with his withering finger.... Back of the house, across a little lane, rises a terraced garden cut out of the side of the "cerro" or hill, the garden plots sustained by stone walls skillfully planned. Good taste and ample and generous expenditure have combined to make the Chapala residence of the Cardens a wholly admirable residence.[10]

The 1898 rainy season was especially intense and prolonged. The lake level rose so high that for much of the second half of the year (as late as

December), the lower gardens of Villa Tlalocan were completely under water.[11] It was changing times for Carden, too. After initially being told he was being reassigned to Puerto Rico, he was appointed the next British consul in Cuba, effective the following year.

Before he left, Villa Tlalocan was the scene of a flurry of social and political activity. Carden's immediate superior, Sir Henry Neville Dering (Envoy Extraordinary and Minister Plenipotentiary to Mexico, 1894–1900), visited Chapala for tea in February 1899.[12] Other guests at the tea party included Lorenzo Elizaga and his wife, Sofía Romero Rubio de Elizaga (sister-in-law of President Díaz); Roberto de la Mora; Carmen Castillo Rivera de Mora; and Joaquín Cuesta Gallardo.[13]

The Cardens held a farewell party in Chapala shortly before the sale of Villa Tlalocan to Carlos Eisenmann was announced in mid-March.[14] Carden and his wife then donated their small collection of archaeological finds to the National Museum in Mexico City and left for Cuba.[15] Carden would eventually return to Mexico fourteen years later as British Ambassador, his final post in a long career.

Charles Grove Johnson

English engineer and architect Charles Grove Johnson (1865–1942) worked in Mexico from about 1895 to 1931. Johnson first came to Mexico in 1895 to help George Edward King build Villa Tlalocan.[16] Johnson set up his own office as an architect in Mexico City in 1903.[17] He became very interested in pre-Hispanic constructions and published an illustrated article about the ruins of Mitla, Oaxaca, in the *Journal of the Royal Institute of British Architects* in 1904.[18]

Johnson moved in the upper echelons of society in Mexico City and became personal friends with the Cardens, accompanying them part way to the port of Veracruz when they were reassigned from Mexico to Cuba in 1899.

Unlike King, his former partner, who fled the country during the Revolution, Johnson remained in Mexico until the early 1930s.

Johnson worked mainly in Mexico City and played a part in designing and constructing a new British Legation building (later consulate) in Mexico City in 1911 at Rio Lerma #71. He was also responsible for the city's Cowdray Sanatorium (now the American-British-Cowdray Hospital), which opened in 1923.[19]

Johnson had been a resident of Gibraltar for several years when he died in the Moroccan port of Tangier in 1942.

The new owner of Villa Tlalocan, Carlos Eisenmann, was a German-born copper magnate who had emigrated to the US as a teenager in 1872.[20] He subsequently settled in Mexico and was soon moving in the rarified social circles surrounding President Díaz.

Eisenmann made his fortune from mining and land speculation, initially in the remote unsettled central part of the Baja California Peninsula in the 1880s, and later in southern Mexico. He cemented his ties to Baja California by marrying Mulegé-born Amelia Brígida Jordán Aguilar in 1881. That same year, Eisenmann, in partnership with Manuel Tinoco, won a 99-year concession to develop a mining colony called El Boleo.[21] Backed by French investors, they formed the El Boleo Mining Company which built, from the ground up, the port town of Santa Rosalía on the Gulf of California, complete with its offices, railroad, smelter, laboratory, storehouses, customs house, schools and residences.[22] That town's striking French-style architecture dates back to this period.

The rising demand for copper from fledgling electric companies in the US and Europe ensured that copper prices remained high. By 1895 the El Boleo Company accounted for more than 80% of Mexico's exports of copper ingots, making Eisenmann and his partners immensely wealthy.

The Eisenmanns' Mexico City home was on Paseo Reforma. All five of their daughters—ranging in age from Carlota (17) to Blanca (11)— attended a big fancy dress party at the family home in August 1899.[23] Guests at that party included Arturo Braniff and Lorenzo Elizaga's wife, Sonia Romero Rubio de Elizaga. Commenting on their purchase of Villa Tlalocan, one newspaper called the Eisenmanns a "very cultivated family, the daughters being accomplished musicians," and expressed confidence that they "would be a positive addition to the excellent society which, in the season, gathers at Chapala."[24] The family was expected to spend September at their new vacation home:

> The gardeners are now at work trimming the lawns and flower beds. It is to be feared that the wealth of magnificent red roses which now make the garden fragrant will have disappeared by then.[25]

Tragically, less than a year later, the family lost Blanca to typhoid fever. On a happier note, regular visits to Chapala worked their romantic magic on her parents, and Mrs. Eisenmann duly gave birth on 28 January 1903, at their Chapala residence, to yet another daughter: María de los

The Cuesta Gallardo brothers

Manuel Cuesta Gallardo (1873–1920), a godson of President Díaz, and his brother, Joaquín Cuesta Gallardo (1874–1915), were members of a family of wealthy and influential engineers whose business interests ranged from agriculture and irrigation to building the hydro-electric power station between El Salto and Juanacatlán that supplied electricity to Guadalajara.

The family owned several haciendas, including the Hacienda Atequiza, and were responsible for the deplorable draining of the eastern third of Lake Chapala in the first decade of the twentieth century. Between them, Manuel and Joaquín amassed an astonishing 87,000 hectares {215,000 acres} of farmland.

Joaquín and his wife, Antonia Moreno Corcuera (c1878–1958) purchased the now-ruined "Hacienda La Maltaraña" at the eastern end of the lake, near La Barca. This beautiful building, originally known as Villa Cristina, had been designed by Guillermo de Alba for José G. Castellanos and his wife, Cristina.

Ángeles. A local official, Felipe Dávalos, visited Villa Tlalocan three days later to record the birth, a clear mark of the respect in which the family was held.

After the Eisenmanns, Villa Tlalocan was acquired by Manuel Cuesta Gallardo. Several sources claim that he bought the property in 1908 from Eisenmann's estate.[26] However, though I have failed to establish when the house changed hands or when Eisenmann died, he was most certainly still alive in 1910, when both he and his wife attended the ceremony in Mexico City at which their eldest daughter, Carlota, married Kansas native Albert Curtis Taylor (1871–1918).

Regardless of precisely when Manuel Cuesta Gallardo acquired Villa Tlalocan, he allegedly did so intending to build a vacation home there as a gift for President Díaz. In 1911, in the early stages of the Mexican Revolution, Cuesta Gallardo was governor of Jalisco for a short time, before being removed by supporters of Madero. The Revolution thwarted his grandiose business dreams and his plans for Villa Tlalocan.

In 1917, with financial problems looming, Manuel Cuesta de Gallardo transferred the title of Villa Tlalocan to a younger sister, Teresa Cuesta viuda de Corcuera.[27] The following year, Manuel was arrested in Mexico City for financial impropriety. The Compañía Hidroeléctrica e Irrigadora de Chapala, which he had co-founded in 1909, and which had issued bonds in Germany in 1910 to "build immense hydroelectric works on the Santiago river and an important power transmission line to mines north west of Guadalajara", was declared bankrupt.[28]

Teresa had several other siblings. In 1925 she sold Villa Tlalocan to two of her brothers, Luis and Enrique Cuesta Gallardo.[29] Seven years later, Luis's share was transferred to his two children, Carlos and Teresa Cuesta Gallardo. After this, the original Villa Tlalocan property was divided into two large sections, separated by the "little lane" that now became part of a new road (the continuation of the former Calle Agua Caliente, now Avenida Hidalgo) that extended west to Villa Montecarlo and El Manglar.[30] The northern section was the terraced garden area sprawling up the hillside. The southern section, which included the main house and formal gardens, was later split into four parts: Villa Ferrara, Villa San José, Villa Tlalocan and Villa Adriana respectively.

The exterior of Villa Tlalocan, built in 1895–96, has survived largely intact to this day.

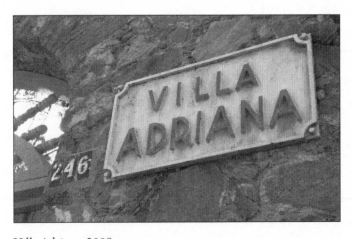

Villa Adriana, 2008.

22

Villa Adriana

West of Tlalocan, at Hidalgo 246, is Villa Adriana, a large property that occupies the final part of the property once owned by Manuel Cuevas, together with a separate adjoining piece of land of different prior ownership.

Villa Adriana was originally designed by Pedro Castellanos and later modified by Luis Barragán.[1] Jesús González Gallo (Jalisco state governor from 1947 to 1953) and his wife, Paz Gortázar, owned the house for a long time. Parties at their vacation home were legendary and Guadalajara architect Juan Palomar still recalls his childhood visits there with Fernando González Gortázar, one of González Gallo's sons:

> I was, in early childhood, one of the guests to the legendary kermises that Doña Paz Gortázar organized every season. The memory of the shaded, mysterious garden, of the sunny meadow, of the stalls and games, of the calm and joyful atmosphere that the entire surroundings transmitted, remains intact to this day.[2]

Villa Adriana, a magnificent building created by two of the region's most famous architects, has been impeccably maintained to this day. The property has twin piers jutting out into the lake, an obvious landmark on panoramic and aerial photos.

Jesús González Gallo was born in Yahualica, Jalisco, in 1900. After studying in Guadalajara to become a lawyer, he occupied several positions in the state government, including secretary of the supreme court of justice, and served as a criminal and civil judge. He entered politics in 1934 and was Senator of Jalisco from 1934 to 1940. He joined the federal government in 1940 and served as Secretary of the Presidency during the six-year term of President Manuel Ávila Camacho.

He then returned to Guadalajara where he was Governor of Jalisco from 1947–1953. During his term in office he increased the number of civil, financial and Supreme Court judges, and initiated numerous urban and highway modernization projects. These included improvements to the highway between Guadalajara and Chapala, as well as a major remodeling of downtown Chapala. Regrettably, the latter entailed destroying some of the town's oldest buildings to create Avenida Francisco I. Madero. This is also when Playa Chacaltita, the beach east of the pier, was eliminated in order to build the spacious Paseo Ramón Corona, with the area to its south then infilled for use as a lakeshore public park.

González Gallo died in a motor vehicle accident in 1957. The Centro Cultural González Gallo, the museum and exhibition center housed in the former Chapala Railroad Station, is named in his honor.

One of González Gallo's sons, J. Jesús González Gortázar, a lawyer and federal deputy of Jalisco, authored *Aquellos Tiempos en Chapala*, a short, lively account of the history of the lake and the town.[3] Two other sons both became architects and have worked in Chapala: Federico designed the Chapala Yacht Club, and is working to restore the Hotel Arzapalo, while Alejandro built Plaza las Palmas, close to Villa Paz.

Casa Albión (later Villa Josefina), c. 1900. (Anon)

23

Casa Albión (Villa Josefina)

Villa Josefina, at Hidalgo 248, originally had a distinctive cottage appearance. When Septimus Crowe built it in about 1896 as his own home, it was known as Casa Albión.[1] Crowe sold it five years later to the US-born Guadalajara beer magnate Joseph Maximilian Schnaider (1858–1922), known in Mexico as José María Schnaider. Like many other old villas in Chapala, the new owner renamed it after his wife, and it still bears her name to this day.

Crowe had previously built and lived in Villa Montecarlo. After selling the Montecarlo in 1895, he moved a short distance along the lakeshore and began building Villa Albión, purportedly modeled on "the villa of Garibaldi at Capri."[2]

What was Crowe like? A correspondent for *The Mexican Herald* wrote admiringly that,

> Mr. Crowe is a linguist, a scholar and a gentleman of the sort that Old England produces. He has one of the most fascinating homes the ingenuity of man, aided by nature, may produce, and his taste in decoration and in gardening have evoked, as by a magic spell, a lovely and at the same time most English home.[3]

American ethnographer Jeremiah Curtin, who met Crowe by chance on a train in November 1895, thought him "one very peculiar Englishman" and described how he was "dressed in a Spanish Costume: a large Mexican hat trimmed with gold braid; a short, white coat; tight trousers; and a long, red sash; and white gloves."[4]

Contemporary accounts of Casa Albión, which cost "around 5000 to 8000 dollars,"[5] described it as "a pretty Swiss chalet almost overhanging

Joseph Maximilian Schnaider

Joseph Maximilian Schnaider, known in Mexico as José María Schnaider, was born to a German-American couple in St. Louis, Missouri, on 3 April 1858 and married Mary Josephine Erd Mud (1861–1954) in Illinois in 1882.[6] After the birth of their first three children in St. Louis, the couple moved to Monterrey in northern Mexico, where another child was born in 1894. Their final two children were born in Guadalajara.

Schnaider created some of Mexico's most famous beers. After learning his craft in St. Louis, the master brewer moved to Monterrey in 1890 to start Cervecería Cuauhtémoc. That brewery, now part of FEMSA (Fomento Mexicano), produced its first barrel of Carta Blanca beer in 1893 and won prizes at the Chicago (1893) and Paris (1898) world fairs.

In 1895, Schnaider moved to Guadalajara where he bought La Perla brewery, established five years earlier. With the help of his brother, Walter, he soon transformed it into the largest brewery in the city. Very actively involved in civic affairs, Schnaider was president of the American Club of Guadalajara when it moved to new premises in 1904 so that its more than one hundred members could have larger club rooms and a library.[7]

Schnaider died in the spa of Baden Baden, Germany, on 19 August 1922; the ship carrying his casket back home was lost at sea.

the lake." It had "grassy terraces, a small harbor for his smart yacht; and charming, flower-bedecked piazza," where a "Union Jack floats gaily from the flagstaff."[8] In 1898, Crowe was reported to be enlarging his premises by adding several small apartments.[9]

The pioneering Señor Crowe was also the first person to introduce a European-style sailing boat to Lake Chapala. Having been an enthusiastic sailor in Europe as a young man, he ordered a five-ton yacht from Hamburg, Germany, specifically adapted for Lake Chapala.[10] After *Estrella* ("Star") arrived, one of his principal enjoyments "was to entertain Britishers and other foreigners who visited the lake on board… [and] he was always happy to carry them off for all kinds of cruises."[11]

Crowe's parties were equally memorable affairs, according to artist and author Ixca Farías, who first visited Chapala in the 1880s. Farias recounted his memories of how Crowe held a dance at his home on one occasion at which the music was provided by two harps and a violin; the guests included Gabriela Galván de Saldaña, Maclovia González de Cañedo, María Pacheco de Arzapalo, and Crowe's washerwomen. It was a cool evening, so the host wore a woolen sarape over his formal attire.

On another occasion, Crowe served tea and biscuits (cookies) one autumn afternoon around a bonfire in his garden. By that stage of his life, Crowe disliked late nights and, as Farías recalled, "a bell would ring when it was time for him to retire, as a sign for guests to leave."[12]

Crowe may have persuaded Lionel Carden to build a home in Chapala, but this did not make the two men close friends. This became apparent in May 1897 after Crowe dynamited some "large rocks," presumably to complete work on his private yacht harbor. When Carden complained to the local council that debris from the explosions had damaged the roof of his home, Crowe claimed that no debris had flown more than "10 or 15 meters," and that several eyewitnesses, including Eduardo Collignon and Joseph Hayes, would testify to that effect. Even so, he offered to pay for any damage his work had caused.[13]

After Schnaider bought Villa Albión in 1901, he renamed it Villa Josefina, and soon unveiled a whole series of major plans for Chapala. Between 1902 and 1904, he joined forces with Ignacio Arzapalo and Ernesto Paulsen to start the Jalisco Development Company, advised a company that planned to develop Isla de los Alacranes, and was elected first vice-president of the Chapala Yacht Club.[14] Schnaider also later worked with Salvador Pérez and his son to export the local mineral water.[15]

In February 1916, Schnaider placed Quinta Josefina at the disposal of General Venustiano Carranza, one of the main leaders during the Revolution, who would become the 37th President of Mexico the following year. On 27 February, after meetings in Guadalajara, Carranza, accompanied by his family and entourage, took the train as far as La Junta, from where automobiles transported them to Chapala. They arrived at 3.30pm and locals lined the streets to applaud Carranza as he walked through the town for a late lunch at Villa Josefina. "El Primer Jefe" then relaxed by strolling along the beach.[16] A number of federal and state dignitaries visited him in Chapala over the next few days.

Like many of his contemporaries, Schnaider was desperate for the completion of an all-season road to Chapala. He was an enthusiastic early adopter of the motor car; by 1919, he was President of the Jalisco Automobile Club (Club Automovilistico Jalisciense) which helped build the first all-season road between Guadalajara and Tlaquepaque. Naturally, Chapala was also in the club's sights, though that road was only finished in 1925, shortly after Schnaider's demise.

Villa Josefina, Schnaider's family holiday chalet in Chapala, was regularly pictured on early postcards. It was also the setting for the earliest known moving pictures related to Lake Chapala. In 1922, privately taken shorts, made by Rod Moore and E. P. Hunziker,[17] including footage of the "chalet", were shown at the Guadalajara home of Schnaider's son William (Guillermo).[18]

Schnaider's will left the villa in Chapala to his daughter, María Enriqueta (Nettie) Schnaider (1901–1980). In 1923, a year after her father's death, Nettie married General Miguel Acosta Guajardo (1891–1947), who had served under Carranza as Head of Military Operations for the 5th and 10th districts of Jalisco. The couple allowed Swedish artist Nils Dardel and his partner to use Villa Josefina for several weeks in the early 1940s, while Dardel prepared canvasses for a show in New York.[19]

Villa Josefina remained in the Schnaider family until the start of this century.[20]

* * *

Villa Niza (right) and Villa Elena (left), c. 1930. (Pub: Altamirano)
West of Villa Niza is an earlier residence, Villa Elena, at Hidalgo 258. Shown in photos as early as 1902, it may well be the "handsome stone cottage of two stories near Mr. Crowe's place" that Manuel Henríquez (who worked with Guillermo de Alba) was "putting up" in 1898.[1]

24

Villa Niza

Villa Niza, at Hidalgo 250, is another of the buildings in Chapala designed by Guillermo de Alba. It was built at the request of Andrés Somellera, a Guadalajara businessman, whose ancestors included several enterprising and ultimately successful cousins who first came to Mexico from Spain in the mid-nineteenth century.[2]

The house, which looks more American than European in style, makes the most out of its lakeshore position with a *mirador* (look out) atop the central tower of the structure, which affords sweeping panoramic views over the gardens and lake. De Alba's strong geometric design boasts only minimal exterior ornamentation.

Claims that Villa Niza dates back to 1903 are not correct.[3] Pre-1919 photographs of the shoreline show that Villa Josefina had no immediate neighbor to its west. According to a 1919 newspaper, the "new chalet" being built by Andrés Somellera close to the picturesque Schnaider house was close to completion but not yet finished.[4] The final nail in the coffin for any earlier date comes from a 1919 map showing the villas along the lakeshore and their potential federal zone concessions.[5] The entire area between Villa Josefina (Hidalgo 248) and Villa Elena (Hidalgo 258) is clearly marked as *baldío* ("empty lot").

Guillermo de Alba was in the habit of personally photographing buildings he designed soon after their completion; his photo of Villa Niza is signed and dated 1919.[6]

Villa Niza was later owned by Oscar Newton[7] before being acquired in the 1960s by Dr. Salvador Urzúa and his wife, Patricia. Villa Niza has been well maintained over the years and retains many of its original interior features.

The property immediately west of Villa Niza remained vacant and undeveloped until the 1940s. Doña Paz Gortázar (wife of Jesús González Gallo) bought it from Guillermo de Alba in 1935 and sold it six years later to Enrique Anisz (1896–1946).[8] Anisz, born in Lubisa, Czechoslovakia, was a successful businessman in Guadalajara who was instrumental in getting the Celanese Mexicana chemical plant established in Ocotlán. He also organized the Union Forestal de Jalisco y Colima that supplied raw material to the paper mill in Atenquique, where a primary school is named in his honor.

Jardín del Mago, 2019.

25

Jardín del Mago

Further west on Hidalgo, on the mountain side of the street, is a property known as "Jardín del Mago" (Hidalgo 251). A stone dog guards the gate of this interesting property that owes its importance to its strong ties to Luis Barragán. The garden and residence were owned by Barragán's sister, Luz, and her husband, *Don* Mago, an antiquities dealer based in Guadalajara, and date to about 1942.

Barragán considered himself first and foremost a landscape architect and this property, in the words of Guadalajara architect Juan Palomar, is "one of the most important Mexican gardens of all time."[1] Barragán personally oversaw the creation of the extensive terraces and plantings covering around 5000 square meters of the lower slopes of Cerro San Miguel. The multilevel residence is simple and functionalist. Both grounds and home offer constant surprises of vistas and spaces. The upper parts of the property offer exceptional views over the lake.

The work is a key link, in style and date, between the gardens of Ferdinand Bac (under whom Barragán studied in Europe in 1922) and Barragán's own internationally-acclaimed Jardines del Pedregal de San Ángel (1948) in Mexico City. The Jardin del Mago is an intermediate step showing how Barragán had begun to develop his own individual style that would later make him world famous.[2]

Barragán's multiple links with Chapala are a vitally-important, yet often overlooked, element of the town's cultural heritage. While the property and gardens appear currently to be in good hands, they deserve stronger municipal, state and federal protection.

Villa Reynera, c. 1925. (Anon)

26

Villa Reynera

Precisely when Villa Reynera (Hidalgo 266A) was built, or who built it, or even who first owned it, is unclear. Early photos show "Reynera" emblazoned on the side of the tower, between the second and third stories;[1] the alternative spelling of Villa Reinera appears on the entrance today.

The original three-story building, which no longer exists, was probably built in the first decade of the twentieth century.[2] It was an imposing, Victorian-style structure with high ceilings and numerous bay windows. Ground floor rooms opened onto a broad covered terrace that hugged the lake side of the house. Eschewing symmetry, the architect added an unusual steeply-pitched conical roof atop the home's southwest corner. The slight architectural similarities to Casa Braniff, designed by English architect George King, suggest that Villa Reynera might also have been the work of King or one of his associates.

Villa Reynera's claim to fame, aside from its distinctive architecture, is that the so-called "Russian dancers"—Zara Alexeyewa (born Eleanore Saenger) and her dancing partner, Holger Mehnen— lived here while they prepared for a performance in the Degollado Theater, Guadalajara, in January 1925.[3] This was the beginning of a close association with Chapala and Ajijic that would last the rest of their lives.

Zara and Holger were on their way back to the US from a tour of Europe and South America when they arrived in Guadalajara, learned about Chapala, and decided to stay at Lake Chapala for several months. Their decision proved to be a productive one, particularly for Zara. Much later in life, she recalled how it was on a moonlit night at Villa Reynera that she got the inspiration for two original ballets: *Princess of the Moon*, which she composed the following day, and *Nauollin*.[4] It would be more than half a century before either ballet was performed in public.[5]

The two dancers led a most adventurous life. In July 1925, only a few months after performing at the Degollado Theater, Zara wrote from the Villa Reynera to a friend in Los Angeles, sharing her adventures looking for buried treasure, and admitting that she and Holger had lost money in a "disastrous mining venture."[6]

Zara and Holger left Mexico later that summer to visit her family in New York, where they became devotees of the self-realization movement led by Swami Paramahansa Yogananda. After the death of her father in 1929, Zara asked the Swami to accompany her when she returned to Chapala with her mother and Holger.[7] The iconic photograph of the Swami, standing arms aloft on a broad-sailed boat in the middle of the lake, that is still regularly used in self-realization publicity materials today, was taken during this trip.

Zara and Holger continued to live in Villa Reynera during the 1930s while the dancing partners fought to extract some profit from the gold mine they had bought in the hills above Ajijic. According to American travel writer Neill James, who moved to Ajijic in 1943,

> The two handsome dancers on horseback, the girl clad in red Bavarian riding costume, flowing sleeves, wearing ballet slippers and a sombrero astride Tony her black horse, were an exotic sight as they galloped down the Camino Real carrying gold dust in saddle bags to Chapala.[8]

The many adventures and mishaps they had while trying to make a go of their mine are recounted in Zara's fictionalized autobiography, *Quilocho and the Dancing Stars*, which also includes numerous references to Villa Reynera.[9]

A tragic accident in 1936, shortly before a scheduled performance in Guadalajara, cost Holger the use of his legs; he never danced again, never fully recovered, and died in 1944, by which time Zara and her mother had left Villa Reynera and moved to Ajijic.[10]

In her later years Zara was an ardent environmentalist. She was one of the most active campaigners in the foreign community supporting the "Save the Lake" movement that arose when lake levels plummeted during the severe drought of the 1950s. The indomitable Zara, a force to be reckoned with, passed away on 12 January 1989.

According to Natalia Cuevas, the original old mansion of La Reynera was demolished and replaced with a more modern construction.[11] This may have been in 1946 when there is an unconfirmed report that the villa with its extensive grounds was bought, subdivided and sold on.

A short distance west of Villa Reynera, on the other side of the highway, a short, dead-end side street climbs towards Cerro San Miguel. This otherwise unremarkable street is Callejón Mr. Crowe, named after Septimus Crowe.[12]

Still further west, another steep side street, Calle Lourdes, leads directly up the hillside to La Capilla de Lourdes.

Capilla de Lourdes, c. 1943. (J. González)
After the consecration of Capilla de Lourdes in August 1941 this part of Chapala,
previously known as Barrio del Ixtle, became known as Barrio de Lourdes.

27

La Capilla de Lourdes

Calle Lourdes was formerly lined with palm trees and known as La Calzada de las Palmas. It was paid for by Aurelio González Hermosillo, who owned Villa Montecarlo, and built in 1909 by Guillermo de Alba. Between 1903 and 1907, González Hermosillo amassed a huge tract of land on this hillside by purchasing land from at least a dozen different individuals.[1] On the final day of 1909 a hill-climbing contest for automobiles was held up the steep new street. The winner, which made it all the way to the top, was a German-made Protos with five passengers driven by Benjamín Hurtado.[2]

After Guillermo González Hermosillo y Brizuela inherited Villa Montecarlo from his father in the 1930s, he helped build La Capilla de Lourdes at the top of the street, on land donated by Walter Schnaider.[3] Schnaider also financed the chapel's tower, in memory of "his brother José M. Schnaider who had loved Chapala so much."[4] The first stone was laid on 18 March 1940 and the chapel, designed by Juan Palomar y Arias and engineer Luis Ugarte,[5] was consecrated in August the following year.

With the support of the parish priest and author, Antonio de Alba, the project was largely funded by prominent Guadalajara families who owned vacation homes and enjoyed the healthy Lourdes-like spa water at Lake Chapala. These individuals included Guillermo González Hermosillo y Brizuela; María de la Luz Brizuela; Agustín Troutier and his wife, Concepción Ibarra; Walter Schnaider and his wife, María Ancira; Amparo Martínez; and Guadalupe Gallardo.[6]

Unfortunately, this part of the hillside is notoriously unstable; even extensive later restoration work by Ugarte has failed to prevent continued deterioration of this significant historical and cultural landmark.

Juan Palomar y Arias

Guadalajara architect and educator Juan Palomar y Arias (1894–1987) maintained enormous pride in his native city and was regarded by Luis Barragán as having the most accurate aesthetic eye in the city. Palomar was a modernist architect who fought all his life to make the city a better place in which to live.[7]

In the 1930s he collaborated with Pedro Castellanos on the ambitious plan, never realized, called "El Plan Loco" ("The Mad Plan") for a futuristic Guadalajara.[8]

Palomar played a part in numerous urban planning projects in Guadalajara and in many transcendental works. He combined his architecture practice with teaching at all three major Guadalajara universities: the University of Guadalajara, ITESO, and the Autonomous University of Guadalajara.

Villa Montecarlo, c. 1908. (Anon)

28

Hotel Villa Montecarlo

With its main entrance on Calle Lourdes, the Hotel Villa Montecarlo (Hidalgo 296) has extensive gardens, facilities and pools overlooking the lake. Despite its undistinguished modern buildings, this property has one of the most interesting histories of any in Chapala and remains a charming place to visit.

Separating historical fact from fantasy is especially challenging in the case of Villa Montecarlo. The legend, regularly retold as fact, has Septimus Crowe visiting Chapala and building Villa Montecarlo in 1896. But, as I suggested in the introduction, Crowe's house was described as early as 1893 and may well have been built several years earlier, perhaps only shortly after he first arrived in Mexico in about 1885.

Whenever it was that Crowe first saw Lake Chapala, it was probably love at first sight. It is easy to imagine him strolling west of the church and finding this grassy knoll with its incredible view over the lake. As a keen yachtsman, Crowe must have been absolutely thrilled at the prospect of exploring such a long and beautiful shoreline by boat. He bought the property (it is unclear from whom) and erected an imported, prefabricated wooden chalet on the highest point of the site, naming it Monte Carlo (now spelled locally as a single word), presumably because of how much it reminded him of the Mediterranean.

As more foreigners settled in Chapala, Crowe saw the opportunity to sell Villa Montecarlo and build himself a new home, Casa Albión, right on the lake, with a small private harbor for his yacht. Accordingly, he sold Villa Montecarlo in 1895 to Cora Alice Townsend de Rascón, the widow of wealthy hacienda owner and diplomat José Martín Rascón, the first Mexican minister to Japan.[1]

Septimus Crowe

Septimus Crowe (1842–1903) was born on 29 June 1842 in Kåfjord, a copper-mining town in the extreme north of Norway. He was the youngest of eighteen children born to the two wives of John Rice Crowe. Septimus's mother died when he was only a year old. A year and a half later, when his father was appointed British consul, the family moved to Christiania (now Oslo).

As a young man, Crowe spent several years in Glasgow, Scotland, as a clerk with a shipping firm. An avid yachtsman, Crowe later bought his own yacht to sail around Scandinavia. In 1864 he began working alongside his father in Christiania and was appointed British vice-consul there in 1872. After his father retired in 1875, Septimus served more than once as acting consul general between permanent appointees. Several of his brothers and half-brothers also became British diplomats around the world.

The Crowes lived next door in Norway to George Parker Bidder, a wealthy British railroad engineer and his family. Septimus married Bidder's daughter, Georgina, in 1874, and the couple had their only child, a son, the following year.

In about 1883, Crowe suddenly abandoned everything, including his wife and son, to begin a new life. His eight-year-old son was told that his father had died, and never learned the truth.[2]

Crowe moved to Mexico just as diplomatic relations between the UK and Mexico were being renewed in 1884. His new life revolved around mining and Lake Chapala. He joined a British syndicate that bought and operated a mine in Mezquital del Oro, eighty-five kilometers north of Guadalajara, and became its financial director.[3] Declining reserves of ore led to layoffs in 1896; a disastrous storm and mudslide later that year ended the mine's hopes of recovery.[4]

Crowe built several houses in Chapala, including Villa Montecarlo, Villa Josefina and Villa Bell/Bela, and encouraged his friends to move there. Septimus Crowe was in Mexico City on his way to the UK in July 1903 when he was taken ill and died of pneumonia.

Following her husband's sudden death in 1893, Cora managed the family haciendas in San Luis Potosí single-handedly with considerable success. She bought Villa Montecarlo as a Christmas gift for her parents: Mary Ashley Townsend, a well-known New Orleans poet, and her husband, Gideon.[5] Cora and her mother had both attended the 11th Congreso Internacional de Americanistas in Mexico City earlier that year, as had British consul Lionel Carden, who had, by then, started his own well-appointed home in Chapala, Villa Tlalocan.[6]

Cora's parents spent several months each winter in Chapala. Mr. Townsend, who liked it "for the sake of his health,"[7] planted dozens of coffee trees. The Townsend house, the "furthest west of all the cottages",[8] remained a prominent local landmark:

> On the highest peak one sees a bright red and white house with a tower which looks as if it came from the old baronial castles of the middle ages.[9]

Tragedy befell the Townsends. Gideon died in 1899.[10] Only two years later, Mary Ashley Townsend was severely injured in a train crash on her way to Mexico and she died a few months later.[11]

What became of the Montecarlo property? Later records prove that it was eventually acquired by Aurelio González Hermosillo (1862–1927), a wealthy lawyer and financier who owned the Hacienda Santa Cruz del Valle near Guadalajara. But the conflicting versions of how this occurred are impossible to reconcile and leave several unanswered questions.

According to his granddaughter, Lorenza González Hermosillo de Martínez, Aurelio González Hermosillo bought all the property—"from the top of the hill to the shore of the lake"—from Mr. Crowe. This led to the whole area becoming known at the start of the century as the colonia Hermosillo. In fact, Crowe had sold the Villa Montecarlo several years earlier and the property was acquired between 1903 and 1907 in multiple transactions, none of which involved Crowe, who had died unexpectedly in Mexico City in 1903 while en route to England with every intention of returning.

Nor is it likely that González Hermosillo bought the property from the Townsends, as is claimed by American journalist George Wythe Baylor, who, after visiting family in Guadalajara in 1902, wrote that Mrs. Townsend had "just" sold the property to González Hermosillo.[12] Mary Ashley Townsend had died the year before and still owned the Montecarlo at the time of her death.[13] Her passing was as unexpected as Crowe's own demise. Moreover, in 1904, when her estate was being wound up, *The Jalisco Times* reported that,

> A small tract of land and its buildings, known as the "Monte Carlo," situated in Agua Caliente street, this town, will be sold at auction

for taxes about the middle of next month. It is registered as belonging to Mrs. Maria Ashley Van Voorish, widow of Townsend, and is appraised at $1,500 value.[14]

In about 1904, regardless of how he became the owner, Aurelio González Hermosillo set about replacing the existing "Townsend" home with a much more elaborate residence. A year later, with the new house still under construction, he was granted a ten-year exemption from municipal and state taxes "for the house he is building named Villa Monte Carlo."[15]

According to the popular version, González Hermosillo tore down the original house to build himself a new Italian-style house, designed by Italian architect Angelo Corsi; González Hermosillo contracted the architect in Italy and then imported Italian furnishings and works of art to complete his home.[16]

Angelo Corsi

According to his marriage certificate, Italian engineer-architect Angelo Corsi (Angel Corsi in Mexico), born in about 1867, first moved to Guadalajara in about 1897. Corsi's name has been associated (rightly or wrongly) with several projects in Chapala, including the Villa Ana Victoria (built before he arrived in Mexico), Villa Montecarlo and Villa Macedonia.

Corsi's commissions in Guadalajara included family homes for Aurelio González Hermosillo, built in 1900, and Julio Collignon, built prior to 1905.[17] Corsi is best known, however, for being the architect of the "Belle Époque" Teatro Saucedo in Puerto Vallarta, completed in 1922. It was that city's first theater and later became its first hotel.[18]

In 1899, soon after arriving in Guadalajara, Corsi was contracted to build the first of four public schools in the city, for which the local government had budgeted $200,000. The school, for girls, had 6 classrooms, a house for the principal, and had gardens for a "kindergarten, military exercises and recreation."[19]

Corsi developed excellent political connections and became the right-hand man of José Rolleri, the Italian consul in Guadalajara.[20] Corsi was given the responsibility in 1907 of decorating the Government Palace for a banquet for the state governor, Miguel Ahumada.[21]

In 1923, Corsi, then aged 56, married María Vicenta Ríos, a 23-year-old Tapatía, in Tlaquepaque. He remained an active member of the Italian community in Guadalajara into the mid-1930s.

There is, however, no independent evidence for the details in this family-history version. Given that Corsi had moved to Jalisco in 1899, it is far more likely that any contract with González Hermosillo was agreed in Guadalajara.

Furthermore, no documentary evidence has surfaced linking Corsi to the 1905–1906 reconstruction. He was, however, responsible for the major remodeling of Villa Montecarlo undertaken more than a decade later, in 1918.[22] He was still based in Chapala the following year, working temporarily out of the Hotel Palmera,[23] while he completed his work on Villa Montecarlo and perhaps starting to build Villa Macedonia.

How did González Hermosillo acquire the fittings and furniture for Villa Montecarlo? According to the most-popular version, he traveled with his family to Venice in 1901, bought the Palazzo Grimani—complete with all its antique furnishings—and then shipped everything back to Mexico to decorate the family's various homes.[24] The items from this trip later displayed at Villa Montecarlo included a pair of terracotta lions and an Italianate statue of a female figure.

The details of this extravagant shopping trip are appealing, but inaccurate. Passenger manifests and photographs show that the major family trip to Europe was in 1912, not 1901. More significantly, there is no record of any member of the family ever buying either of the two palaces of that name in Venice, even if they did return with many period furnishings.

Factual details aside, Corsi's 1918 remodeling of Villa Montecarlo resulted in a most impressive building, Italianate in style, grand in concept, and set amidst beautifully-landscaped gardens. The architect himself is credited with planting the property's huge, shade-giving Indian laurel tree.

Given its splendor, Villa Montecarlo was a fitting choice, therefore, in June 1925 for the honeymoon of Guillermo González Hermosillo y Brizuela (the son of Aurelio González Hermosillo) and his new bride, Cecilia Prieto Menocal, following their wedding in Guadalajara.[25]

On Aurelio González Hermosillo's death two years later, Villa Montecarlo was inherited by his widow, María Josefina Brizuela, prior to being purchased from her in 1935 by their son, Guillermo.[26]

Villa Montecarlo was a regular destination in the 1930s for groups visiting Chapala. For example, in 1932, the Club Alemán (German Club) of Guadalajara drove out to the Montecarlo for a banquet.[27] Two years later, delegates attending a Banking Convention in Guadalajara enjoyed a day trip to the "Quinta Montecarlo" for lunch.[28]

Villa Montecarlo, c. 1945. (J. González)

Jalisco State governor Everardo Topete attended a banquet there in 1935, and must have been suitably impressed. A few weeks later he held a lunch at Villa Montecarlo for a large number of accredited diplomats who were visiting Guadalajara.[29] The guests—including the US Ambassador to Mexico, Josephus Daniels, and his wife, as well as several other ambassadors and their ladies—drove to Chapala and were ferried to Villa Montecarlo in launches. Lunch, which included the local specialty, *caldo michi*, was accompanied by mariachi music and a jazz band. The afternoon concluded with a presentation of folk dancing. The first cars left Chapala for the return drive to Guadalajara at 6.00pm; Governor Topete left much later because his boatman had wandered off during lunch.

In the 1940s, Villa Montecarlo became closely associated with artists and writers. Famous Swedish painter Nils Dardel, who had previously stayed in Villa Josefina, rented Villa Montecarlo for several months in 1941 and wrote delightedly to friends that the garden was the largest and most beautiful in all of Chapala.[30] A few years later, Villa Montecarlo began opening, at least part of each year, as a hotel.

The German-English author Sybille Bedford visited the Montecarlo in 1946–47, while traveling in Mexico with her close friend Esther Murphy Arthur. There is strong circumstantial evidence that the Don Otavio so eloquently portrayed by Bedford in her impressionistic travelogue, *A Visit to Don Otavio*,[31] was based on "Guille Hermosillo," as he was known to his friends. One of Guillermo's family recalls having been told that both women stayed at Villa Montecarlo and maintains that the descriptions of Don Otavio in the book are a completely life-like portrayal of Guille Hermosillo, leaving no doubt that he was the basis for Bedford's character.[32] Parts of the description of the hacienda in the book also match Villa Montecarlo.

Villa Montecarlo was the venue for several important art exhibitions in the 1940s. Opening cocktail parties brought out all the local celebrities of the time, such as authors Nigel Stansbury Millet and Neill James, poet Witter Bynner, artists Sylvia Fein, Ernesto Butterlin, Otto Butterlin, Edythe Wallach, Betty Binkley and Ann Medalie, and Herbert and Georgette Johnson, the first English couple to settle in Ajijic.[33] Like Dardel, both Wallach and Fein later showed their Lake Chapala paintings in solo exhibitions in New York.

Important lunches and other events continued to be held at Villa Montecarlo. In April 1947, Walter Thurston, recently appointed as US Ambassador to Mexico, held a lunch there. The following February, Jalisco State governor J. Jesús González Gallo chose the Montecarlo for a banquet celebrating his first year in office.[34]

By the 1950s, Villa Montecarlo had become one of Chapala's established hotels, listed in all the national guidebooks, and had added several small bungalows for long-term guests, mainly American retirees.[35] When the hotel eventually ran into difficulties and was sold, the original building was torn down and replaced by a generic modern hotel.[36]

The revamped Villa Montecarlo, owned by Nacional Hotelera, S.A., reopened in 1964, just in time for the arrival of two important international groups: HRH Prince Philip, Duke of Edinburgh, plus entourage, who enjoyed a buffet lunch hosted by state officials; and the executive board of People to People, a program founded in 1956 by President Dwight D. Eisenhower as part of the United States Information Agency. Eisenhower was represented by his son, John D. Eisenhower. Also present were President Adolfo López Mateos, former president Miguel Alemán, Jalisco governor Juan Gil Preciado and Walt Disney, a keynote speaker at the lunch, who claimed "Jalisco" was his favorite song.[37]

Villa Montecarlo alternated in the 1970s between being a private members-only club and a hotel-conference center, before being acquired at the end of 1977 by the Universidad de Guadalajara.[38] Since that time the university has made substantial alterations to the buildings and grounds while operating the hotel as Chapala's only large-capacity conference venue.

It is well worth visiting this iconic property to walk in the footsteps of the extraordinary English eccentric Septimus Crowe. Sitting in the shade of the giant old laurel tree, planted more than a century ago, and enjoying the same view that convinced him to spend the rest of his life here, it is easy to appreciate why he beseeched his friends to join him in transforming this once remote fishing village into Mexico's first tourist mecca.

Villa Bela (formerly Villa Bell), 2017.

29

Villa Bela (Villa Bell)

Villa Bela (Lourdes 1) occupies a lakefront lot on the east side of Calle Lourdes, the small street that was built in 1909 and provides access to, and parking space for, the Hotel Montecarlo.

This villa was, I believe, formerly called Villa Bell and built in about 1901 by Septimus Crowe. It was his third residence at Chapala, after selling Villa Montecarlo to Cora Townsend in 1895 and Villa Albión to Joseph Schnaider in 1901.

It is unclear if Crowe himself named it Villa Bell, or why that name was chosen.[1] But it was certainly known as Villa Bell in 1919, when it appears on an official map of the properties granted concessions to use the federal zone bordering the lake.[2] The same spelling is used by Antonio de Alba in 1954 when he lists the properties built by Crowe; de Alba adds that José Ángel Pulido, the administrator of Chapala Yacht Club, once lived there.[3] At what point, and why, the name was changed to Villa Bela remains a mystery.

The Villa Bela property may once have been significantly larger. Attempts to find the early land transfer details for all the relevant properties have so far failed.[4] Even so, Villa Bela's link to Crowe is shown by one of the earliest entries in its land registry history. The property was originally three separate pieces, all owned at one time by Aurelio González Hermosillo. He bought the first section from Feliciana Antolín in 1903 and another section was adjudicated in his favor from the estate of Romualdo Antolín in 1910. The land documents show he bought the middle section from Georgina Crowe (Septimus Crowe's widow) on 10 August 1904.[5]

Crowe's descendants were totally astonished when they learned this only a few months after they had visited Chapala (in 2017) to walk the same streets Septimus had strolled along more than a century before. Septimus had walked out on his wife and son decades before his death, and the family remains convinced that Georgina never visited Mexico, so how it is possible that she came to own or sell this piece of land in Chapala remains a mystery. If the original documents relating to her sale of the property can ever be found, they may offer some interesting clues.

It is possible that Villa Bell was not the last house built by Crowe in Chapala. The local correspondent for *The Mexican Herald* claimed in 1902, a year before Crowe died, that this energetic Englishman was "building a house with an observatory [and a 30-foot telescope] on our bluffs."[6]

La Casita Blanca, 2019.

30

La Casita Blanca

The Little White House, at Hidalgo 298, was the home in the 1950s and 1960s of retired chemist William Warren Rhodes (1888-1968) and his third wife, Harriet (1908-1970).

Rhodes, a graduate of the University of Pennsylvania, worked for over thirty years at DuPont, where he and a colleague developed the chlorofluorocarbon known as Freon. Rhodes became sales manager for aerosol propellants for Kinetic Chemicals, a DuPont subsidiary.

Rhodes was a well-known horseman and maintained his own stables. Always impeccably attired, he was listed in 1939, alongside Douglas Fairbanks, Jr., in the "10 best-dressed men in America."[1]

After he retired in July 1949, Rhodes divorced his second wife and proposed to Harriet Mason. They married in March 1950, moved to Mexico two years later, and lived the remainder of their lives there.[2]

In 1957, Rhodes was photographed by Leonard McCombe for his *Life* magazine article about the Chapala area's expatriates who "settle down to live and loaf in Mexico."[3] McCombe's striking images of life at Lake Chapala, divided the foreign community into two groups: the bridge-playing "older upper crust" and the "younger crew of bohemians."

Rhodes and his wife belonged to the former group, as did pianist Elsa Campbell and her three siblings, and the high-living Williams family. The most famous member of this group was Neill James—photographed overseeing a hunt for buried treasure in Ajijic with a metal detector—who "writes books, builds and rents houses, runs a dress shop and organizes local charities."

Among the expatriates in the younger bohemian set, almost all of whom lived in Ajijic, were Margaret North de Butterlin, who ran an art gallery there; author, educator and translator John Upton; artist Lothar Wuerslin; dress-maker Colleen Wood; and nine-fingered former concert violinist John Langley.

Rhodes died in hospital in Guadalajara in 1968. He left a significant part of his estate to the University of Pennsylvania for a professorship in chemistry, as did his colleague Robert J Thompson. The Rhodes-Thompson Chair was established in 1972.

Harriet Rhodes, who died at home in Chapala two years later, had her own local claim to fame. In 1966 an informal knitting group in the town completed a record 1100 sweaters, as well as 25 baby blankets for needy children; Harriet knitted 90 garments, more than any other foreigner in the campaign.[4]

Villa Virginia, c. 1930. (Pub: F. Martin)

31

Villa Virginia

At Hidalgo 300, Villa Virginia—now known as La Casa Negra de los Garciadiego—was built by Victor and Elizabeth Hunton and dates back to 1905. Several subsequent generations of the Hunton family have also lived in Chapala and Ajijic.

Like the majority of the lakefront properties west of Villa Ferrara, Villa Virginia was originally much closer to the edge of the lake than it is today. The gardens of these properties were enlarged over the years by reclaiming parts of the beach whenever lake levels fell.

Before moving to Mexico, Victor James Hunton (born in London, England, on 14 August 1862) was employed as a clerk on the Great Western Railway. He then worked in Guadalajara as an agent for the Lewis Company of Mexico, until the company transferred him in 1897 to the capital to "assume more important duties."[1] The Lewis Company mined gold, silver, lead and copper and had branch offices in several states for purchasing ores and selling mining supplies.

Victor married Elizabeth Shields Saunders in 1901 at a ceremony in her home state of Virginia. The couple may have first met when Victor was in the US on mining business. Elizabeth, born in 1871, was a British citizen by virtue of her parents: the wonderfully-named couple, Crocket Ynglis Saunders and Theodosia Callaway.[2]

After their marriage, Victor and Elizabeth moved to Aguascalientes, where Victor was appointed as secretary of the Aguascalientes Metal Company, which operated mines in Asientos producing gold, silver and copper. The company's general manager was Albert Doerr (1870–1948), whose son and daughter-in-law tried to revive the mine in the 1950s; their adventures are the basis for the acclaimed novel *Stones for Ibarra*.[3]

Victor Hunton diversified his business interests in 1902 by joining with two partners to win a multiyear contract to supply electricity to the city of Aguascalientes.[4]

Given their common interest in mining, it is more than possible that Victor Hunton knew Septimus Crowe. Perhaps it was Crowe who told him about Chapala. However, Crowe had died by the time the Huntons bought a lakeshore plot of land in 1905 from Sebastian Sainz and María Stephenson (sister-in-law of Eduard Collignon) on which to build their family home.[5]

The Huntons named their house Villa Virginia, after Elizabeth's home state. The couple already had two young daughters—Inés and Dolores—when they moved to Chapala. A third child, José ("Pepe"), arrived in February 1906, shortly after they moved, and Victoría Elizabeth McCullough Hunton ("Isabel" or "Isabela") was born the following year.

Victor commuted regularly to his work in Aguascalientes, leaving his wife and children to live full-time at the lake. As his career progressed, he became an auditor for several other mining companies in western Mexico. He also helped Aurelio González Hermosillo register a claim to a silver-gold vein in Ajijic in 1911;[6] this property is believed to be the one bought in the 1920s by Zara and Holger (of Villa Reynera).

Though its architect is unknown, the style of Villa Virginia displays some superficial similarities with Casa Braniff (of similar age and designed by George E. King) and Villa Reynera. To design Villa Virginia, Hunton may have worked with King (a fellow Brit) or one of his colleagues.

When the Huntons' oldest children reached school age, the well-to-do family employed a private governess, brought over from England. Miss Grace Sydenham Eager, the daughter of a prominent British surgeon, was aged 34 when she accepted the post in 1909.[7]

She had only been in Mexico a few weeks when she and 7-year-old Inés, the Huntons' first-born child, lost their lives in a terrible accident. According to the most detailed account of the event, they were swimming in the lake on 23 May 1909 when the governess was seized by cramp and got into serious difficulties; in trying to help her, Inés also drowned.[8] Both the young girl and her governess were laid to rest in the Chapala municipal cemetery. The size of Grace Eager's estate was surprisingly large, given that she was employed as a tutor; it was valued for probate at £1185, equivalent to at least $175,000 today.

After this tragedy the Hunton family went into deep mourning, and the black-roofed house became known by locals as Villa Negra or Casa

Negra, a name still used today. As a child, author Katie Goodridge Ingram often visited the house during the 1940s and 1950s. She remembers it as "a Victorian house with a lot of droplets of glass on chandeliers, deep jade uncomfortable sofas, old dark furniture, and old dark curtains.... The roof was black and the outside paint was a dull yellow."[9]

As for the Huntons' other children, nothing more is currently known about Dolores, their second child. Later travel records, which only list the parents and their two youngest children, suggest that perhaps she also died as a child.

The two youngest children—Pepe and Isabel— were home-schooled before being sent away to boarding schools in the UK, returning to Mexico only for their summer vacations. Even so, they both retained close ties to the Chapala area for the remainder of their lives.

Tall, fair-haired Pepe, born in Chapala on 14 February 1906, studied at the School of Mines in Cornwall, England, and became a mining engineer. He worked for the American Smelting and Mining company in Santa Eulalia, Chihuahua, before moving to the mining town of Real del Monte in central Mexico. Real del Monte has numerous English connections and is where the first soccer game in Mexico was played.

Pepe married Lois Louise Bryan, a Colorado girl, and they had three children, the first of whom died in Real del Monte as an infant.[10] Pepe's work later took him to the Philippines. He retired to Chapala and died there on 17 May 1975, survived by his wife, then living in Guadalajara, and a son and a daughter, both living in California.

After boarding school in England, Pepe's sister—Victoría Elizabeth ("Isabel"), born on 11 August 1907—studied at a St. Louis secretarial school before taking a job in Mexico City, where she met Carlos Zeiner Stockfisch (1900–1966), who had recently arrived from Germany to work as a dyes expert for the chemical firm I. G. Farben.[11] It was love at first sight; the couple married and had two children: Charles William and Victoria Elizabeth ("Billy" and "Betty").

Isabel and Pepe's mother, Elizabeth Hunton, continued to live in Villa Virginia, tending her garden, to the day she died at the age of 80 in 1951. By all accounts, she was quite a character: strong-willed, opinionated, and sometimes obstinate. She loved her garden, which gained renown as one of the finest in the region. Mrs. Hunton has the unusual distinction of being the inspiration for the central character in one novel and the supporting character in a second. She became a good friend of poet Witter Bynner. After Arthur Davison Ficke visited Bynner and met Mrs. Hunton, he sat down and wrote his only novel, *Mrs. Morton of Mexico* (1939),[12] set entirely at Chapala, in which the title character is based on Elizabeth Hunton.

Sybille Bedford, in her exquisitely-written *A Visit to Don Otavio*, transformed Mrs. Hunton into Mrs. Rawlston, an elderly widow living alone in a "large, dark, ugly, disheveled house."[13]

When Isabel described her childhood to a journalist in the 1960s, she recalled how any trip to Guadalajara was a real adventure, an expedition that sometimes required close to twenty-four hours, given the stagecoach ride to Atequiza along a rut-filled track, and the fact that the train from there to Guadalajara was often many hours late. When she was young, Villa Virginia had no electricity or running water, and breakfast would not be served until each member of the family had gone down to the lake to fill a demijohn with water. Her mother would occasionally invite the entire American colony to tea. As the number of foreigners living in Chapala grew, it became necessary to serve the guests in groups because her mother only had a dozen Dresden china teacups.[14]

In 1956, Isabel and her husband built the Motel Rancho Isabel at the eastern edge of Ajijic.[15] Isabel was an activist in community affairs throughout her life, campaigning to save the lake, preserve the railroad station, get more school books, and so on.[16] An accomplished horsewoman,

Villas immediately west of Villa Virginia, c. 1945. (Anon)

she was a familiar figure as she rode daily along the shore of the lake. Isabel died in January 1970, doing what she loved, after falling from her horse.

Carlos and Isabel's two children—Billy and Betty—both retained close links to Chapala all their lives. Billy, born in Mexico City in 1937, became an agronomist and was studying for his doctorate in entomology at the University of Massachusetts when he won the 15,000-peso prize offered by Guadalajara daily *El Informador* in 1959 for the best proposal to combat the plague of water hyacinth (*lirio*) on the lake.[17] A program to trial the herbicide he advocated began on 6 October that year on a five-hectare mass of *lirio* east of Chapala.[18]

Billy was also the founding president of the Chapala chapter of Ducks Unlimited, an organization set up to protect migratory birds.[19] His daughter, Maeva, still lives in Chapala.

Billy's sister, Betty, who helped raise Maeva, trained in Guadalajara as a veterinarian and then returned to Chapala to live.[20]

Villa Virginia, aka La Casa Negra, remained in the Hunton family for almost half a century. Victor Hunton died in about 1930. After his wife's death in 1951, the house was inherited by their two children, Isabel and Pepe, who sold it in the mid-1960s to Antonio Pérez Garciadiego. In 1970 the property was acquired by Antonio Pérez Parra and Carlos Salvador Pérez Parra.[21]

Villa Macedonia, c. 1920. (José Edmundo Sánchez)

32

Villa Macedonia and the Schmoll residence

Not far from Villa Virginia were Villa Macedonia and the Ferdinand Schmoll residence (precise addresses undetermined).

Also known as the "Michel y Suárez" house, Villa Macedonia was a distinctive building listed as still under construction in 1919.[1] It was noteworthy for its "pleasant square terrace with a view of the lake, extraordinary eaves and a marvelous tower that looks something like a castle."[2]

Villa Macedonia was reportedly designed by Italian architect Angelo Corsi, who was responsible for various residences in Guadalajara, the Teatro Saucedo in Puerto Vallarta, and for the 1918 remodeling of Villa Montecarlo. The house was built in 1919–20 for "Sres. Michel y Suárez." These individuals were José V. Suárez and his wife, María Guadalupe Michel Díaz, who owned a Guadalajara pharmacy, Droguería Michel y Suárez (later Droguería Occidental), that advertised widely from 1917 into the 1920s, before being totally destroyed by a major fire.[3]

María Guadalupe Michel's decision to build Villa Macedonia may have been triggered by the death in 1918 of her father, Froilan Michel, a well-connected Guadalajara businessman. Perhaps financed by her inheritance, the villa was named in honor of her mother, Macedonia Díaz.

Curiously, the year before he died, Froilan Michel had accompanied his daughter, then aged 30, to a notary to re-register her birth and certify that he was indeed the father of the girl previously registered only as Guadalupe Díaz, and that he recognized the child as his daughter for all legal purposes. This suggests that her parents had separated at about the time of her birth and that Macedonia Díaz had been left to bring up several small children on her own.

Almost next to Villa Macedonia was the "Ferdinand Schmoll resi-dence."[4] German painter Ferdinand Schmoll (1879–1950) and his wife, Carolina Wagner (1877–1951), lived there between 1919 and 1921 before moving to Cadereyta, in the central state of Querétaro, where they started Mexico's best-known cactus farm, now run by one of their great nephews. Schmoll exhibited several paintings of Chapala at the Club Alemán in Guadalajara in 1921.[5]

Villa Tatra, January 2008.

33

Villa Tatra

Villa Tatra, behind the ornately decorated entrance at Hidalgo 310, was the home of General John Paul Ratay (1893–1980) and his wife, Gertrude (1910–1984). This retired American couple were the prime movers behind the establishment of the Casa de Ancianos (Old People's Home) in Chapala, which opened its doors in 1971.

The multilingual general, fluent in eight languages, retired from the military in 1946.[1] Gertrude had studied at Northwestern University and become a medically trained social worker. She was working as a nurse when she met the general on a battlefield during the second world war.

After a small family-only wedding ceremony in Evanston, Illinois, in October 1952, they established their home in Chapala, first at Villa Montecarlo and then at Villa Tatra.

Known for hosting extravagant dinner parties and fiestas for up to a hundred guests at a time, the Ratays were always generous benefactors to the community. They were the principal donors for, and founders of, the Old People's Home, which occupies an extensive, beautifully landscaped property, formerly part of the Hacienda Buenavista, adjacent (perhaps somewhat inappropriately) to the municipal cemetery.

In 1955, General Ratay spearheaded the formation of what became the Lake Chapala Society, and was its first president. He had no time for miscreants. Neill James described, in an unpublished note, how the general, angered by three Ajijic beatniks, ensured they got their comeuppance:

> Three beatniks in Ajijic with a Volkswagen were given to robbing small tires for their auto. They made the mistake of lifting a tire from General Ratay's Jeep and fixing it to their Volks. He had heard about

them and was on the lookout. When he saw a Volks with his very own jeep tire on it travelling along he overtook and crowded it to the side of the road, got out with pistol in hand, held it on the beatniks and forced them to remove his tire which they had stolen, replace it on his Jeep, take their own old tire and put it on the Volks. Then he walked around [their vehicle], firing a shot into each tire, and drove away, leaving the unhappy beatniks and their poor wounded Volks with four flat tires."[2]

El Manglar, undated. (Anon)

34

El Manglar

A kilometer west of Villa Tatra, almost in Riberas del Pilar, is the sprawling estate of El Manglar (Avenida Hidalgo 1240/1250).

This property, built by Lorenzo Elizaga and his wife (President Porfirio Díaz's sister-in-law) at the start of the twentieth century, is historically significant because President Díaz stayed here during several of his visits to Chapala.

Lorenzo Elizaga was a prominent and well-connected lawyer based in Mexico City. He was a close associate of Manuel Cuesta Gallardo, the *hacendado* who was given permission to build an embankment to cut off the eastern third of the lake and drain it for farmland. The parties at El Manglar ("The mango grove") were legendary, especially when the president was guest of honor. According to various sources, Lorenzo Elizaga invented a special cocktail, which he christened El Chato ("snub-nosed"), to serve the president. El Chato was (or became) the nickname for Elizaga's son, an infant at the time, but whether the moniker was first given to the cocktail or the child is anyone's guess. The concoction was soon regularly served at parties at El Manglar and elsewhere in Chapala.[1]

A deep dive into early accounts has failed to identify the ingredients used for an El Chato cocktail, though poet Witter Bynner describes it, from his personal experience in the 1920s, as a sweet Martini made of poor gin and good vermouth.[2]

At one El Manglar party a minor disaster befell Mrs. Hunton (of Villa Virginia) when she was introduced to President Díaz. In her daughter's words, "One night the President popped a bottle of champagne and it stained my mother's prized rose-colored silk dress. The spot wouldn't come out and my mother never forgave him."[3]

How many times did President Díaz visit Chapala? The oft-repeated claim that President Díaz spent every Easter in Chapala from 1904 to 1909 is grossly oversimplified.[4] Díaz did not visit Chapala as many times as commonly believed.

On his first recorded visit to Chapala, in 1896, when Díaz visited Lionel Carden in Villa Tlalocan and then attended a banquet on Mezcala Island, he did not even stay overnight. After the banquet, the president and his party nearly lost their lives when they were caught up in a tremendous storm while trying to get back across the lake in the evening to the presidential train waiting for them at Ocotlán.[5]

Díaz did, though, stay several times with his in-laws in later years. When the president visited Chapala in 1904, he did so, not at Easter, but in January, when he spent a weekend in the village accompanied by his wife, Carmen Romero Rubio y Castelló.[6] However, on that occasion Díaz did not sleep at El Manglar, perhaps because his mother-in-law was staying there! Instead, Díaz was a guest of Eduard Collignon at Villa Ana Victoria.[7] The presidential party traveled on a "special train of three elegant cars" to Atequiza, before taking carriages to Chapala. They arrived on Friday 15 January. Díaz's mother-in-law had already been at El Manglar several weeks, and his son, Captain Porfirio Díaz, had arrived a few days earlier.[8] The Jalisco state governor, Miguel Ahumada, and several prominent businessman, including Ernesto Paulsen, Manuel Cuesta Gallardo, and Pedro and Fernando Somellera, paid courtesy visits to the president over the weekend. Díaz's party returned to Mexico City the following Monday.[9]

The following year (1905), Díaz did indeed spend Easter at Lake Chapala. During that visit, while out hunting one day, the president had rendered immediate assistance to an aide who had been accidentally shot in the head.[10]

There is no evidence for any presidential visit to Chapala in either 1906 or 1907. While the Elizagas and many government officials (including vice-president Ramón Corral, finance secretary José Yves Limantour and Roberto Núñez, a sub-secretary of finance)[11] visited Chapala for Easter week, Díaz himself opted instead—both years—to go hunting near Cuernavaca in Morelos.[12]

On the other hand, Díaz's visit to Chapala for Holy Week in 1908 was widely covered in the press. On that occasion, the presidential party arrived from Ocotlán in motor boats owned by Manuel Cuesta Gallardo and Arturo Braniff. The president and his wife stayed the week at El Manglar.[13] Chapala was abuzz that year with a regatta on the lake, sports events and plans to build a yacht club. The president took a daily swim in the lake and did some hunting.[14] Díaz also enjoyed bathing daily in the Las Delicias thermal pools.[15]

Towards the end of 1908 it was reported that Díaz was hoping to rest for several months at Chapala and that Lorenzo Elizaga was preparing a cottage for him at El Manglar. Work was also underway to build an automobile road linking Chapala to El Manglar, obviating the need for traveling there by boat.[16]

In the event, Díaz must have changed his mind, since he did not return to Chapala until the following year (1909), when he again spent time with his inlaws over Easter.[17] Polish-born author Vitold de Szyszlo was an eye witness to the elite of Mexican society enjoying that year's Holy Week regatta at Lake Chapala:

> The president, in a navy blue suit and wearing a panama hat, was accompanied by his wife, dressed all in black, and his daughter Luz, in an elegant outfit. Among the other representatives of the smart set, come to Chapala for the occasion, were: the eminent finance minister Mr. Yves Limantour, to whom the country owes the consolidation of its foreign credit; Mr. Braniff, a railroad king, of working class origins, and Sr. Moreno, whose revenue reached a fabulous figure.... Also present were Mr. Landa, governor of the state of Mexico, Mr. Ahumada, governor of the state of Jalisco, Mr. Escaudon, governor of the state of Morelos, Messrs. Corcuera, Cuesta, Cosio, Hermosillo, Malo, Del Valle, etc.[18]

The civil unrest in Mexico in 1910 caused Díaz and his wife to spend Easter week in several haciendas (Briseñas, Cumuato, Ibarra and Buenavista) near the eastern end of the lake, close to the railroad station in Ocotlán, from where they could easily return to Mexico City at a moment's notice.[19]

As the Revolution got under way, all plans to develop El Manglar as a presidential retreat were abandoned. In 1911, President Díaz, Lorenzo Elizaga and their respective wives fled to Europe. Díaz died in Paris in 1915 and Elizaga died in Switzerland in the 1920s. Both wives eventually returned to Mexico (in 1934), where Carmen Romero Rubio died ten years later and Sofía in 1968.

Following the Revolution, El Manglar was "acquired" (much of the property is *zona federal,* so used on concession from the federal government) by the four Aguilar Figueroa brothers: Ricardo, Luis, José (who sold his share in the 1930s and built a house in La Floresta, Ajijic) and Manuel (who later purchased Villa Ferrara).[20]

El Manglar was rented for a few months in 1926 by a pair of newly-weds: the American artist Everett Gee Jackson and his wife, Eileen. For the princely sum of $35 a month they shared the "run-down" house, which had "a kitchen with a giant old wood-burning cookstove," with a couple of friends.[21] Jackson described El Manglar's extensive grounds and idiosyncratic decorations:

> In front of the house, a garden with palm trees extended down to a retaining wall at the water's edge, where a pier ran out into the lake. At the end of the pier, stone steps went down into the water.
>
> A wide tile-floored verandah stretched all the way across the front of the house. Behind it, rooms along the front and on two sides enclosed a patio, and at the rear of the patio there was a high wall. Rising up behind it was a great dark grove of mango trees.
>
> Eileen and I took the large music room, with its shining tile floor, for our bedroom. We thought it must have been the old dictator's music room, since it had cupids playing musical instruments painting on the ceiling.[22]

When the lake rose unexpectedly high that summer, flooding the railroad tracks and precipitating the closure of the Chapala–La Capilla rail line, it also threatened El Manglar:

> The water kept rising in the lake until our entire front-yard garden had become a part of the sixty-mile-long lake. The water had not only risen above our retaining wall, but was now threatening to engulf our verandah. Great islands of lirio had floated into the area that had formerly been our pretty garden, and we could see snakes among the floating plants. At night, the sound of frogs' croaking filled the air, and I was beginning to wonder when the mosquitos would arrive.[23]

After El Manglar was sold in the 1960s it was divided into three parts, owned respectively by businessman-politician Jorge Dipp Murad, Leopoldo "Polo" Rubio and Jorge Salcedo. The section owned by Dipp was later subdivided, with José Manuel Vázquez Aldana acquiring the stables and Eduardo Cordero Staufert the remainder.[24]

Known as Hacienda El Manglar by some people today (on account of its size, not historical function), the entire fabulous 5.35-acre property includes its own botanical garden, sculpture garden, art studio and semi-Olympic pool.[25]

Pier (El Muelle), Chapala, c. 1915. (Antonio Mólgora)

Part C

35

Waterfront and original yacht club

The earliest jetty or pier in Chapala probably dates from the mid-nineteenth century, when sternwheelers were plying the waters of Lake Chapala transporting passengers, agricultural produce and other freight to and from the numerous villages around the lake. A stockpile of firewood was maintained on the Chacaltita beach at Chapala to refuel the steamships' boilers.

In 1897, as the Hotel Arzapalo near completion, work began on a new pier in the village, better able to serve local needs. At the same time, Ignacio Arzapalo, Manuel Capetillo and Manuel Enríquez[1] were granted permission to erect bathing huts on the beach in front of the hotel. The council stipulated that the huts must all be similar and "sufficiently elegant to beautify the town." They set monthly fees of 25 cents for Arzapalo and Capetillo, with the proviso that their huts were for family use only, and 75 cents for the huts for public use belonging to Enríquez.[2]

In April 1898 the state government gave Chapala $200.00 towards completing the project. The pier, 12 meters wide and 72 meters in length, with trees providing shade and numerous benches, was ready in time for the Independence Day celebrations that September.[3]

A decade later, Guillermo de Alba was entrusted with adding steps to the east side of the "old jetty", and with renovating it and its surrounds.[4] This reference to "old jetty" in 1908 is because that was the year when the Chapala Yacht Club opened a second, much longer pier, made of wood.

The Chapala Yacht Club has a lengthy history. The visionaries behind the first attempt to form a club, in June 1904, were powerful and well-connected individuals: state governor Miguel Ahumada, José María Schnaider, Aurelio González Hermosillo, Luis Pérez Verdía,

Eduard Collignon, T. J. Pomeroy, Manuel Cuesta Gallardo and Ignacio Arzapalo.[5] On their instructions, architect Charles L. Strange drew up plans for a 100-meter-long pier leading to a boathouse and clubhouse. Despite being well-funded, this attempt floundered, partly because of an economic downturn in Guadalajara.[6]

Chapala Yacht Club, c. 1915. (J. R. G.)

Plans for a Chapala sailing club were revived in 1910 by Christian Schjetnan. The founder members of this iteration of the Chapala Yacht Club included several federal politicians, powerful businessmen, the leading lights of Guadalajara society, and British peer and politician William Montagu (1877–1947), the 9th Duke of Manchester. The duke and his wife had visited Chapala previously (in 1905) and the duke donated the main trophy for the club's 1910 regatta.[7]

The club had more than 130 members when it inaugurated its wooden clubhouse on 9 April 1911. Unfortunately, by that time, political unrest meant that the many stakeholders who had close ties to the Díaz regime were unwilling to take any active part in proceedings. The wooden clubhouse, built on metal posts at the end of the pier, had offices, a library, ballroom, casino, restaurant, terraces, a lookout and a lighthouse (which never worked). All the furnishings were imported, even down to the flatware and tablecloths. The club also imported three sailboats, none of which stayed afloat for long. The *Condor*, about sixty feet long, was eventually abandoned in Ajijic; the *Oslo* and the *Urca* both ran aground on Scorpion Island.[8]

By 1914, with the Mexican Revolution still disrupting life in Mexico, the yacht club had been abandoned. On 18 November 1916 it burned down. According to local lore, Rafael Barajas, a young Chapala boy thwarted in love, was standing by the building when he decided to make a fresh start. He set fire to his former love's letters, threw them over his shoulder and never looked back. Unfortunately, the burning papers set the wooden yacht club ablaze. Luckily for Barajas, five witnesses came forward after his arrest to support his claim that it was an unfortunate accident.[9]

The series of piers in Chapala's history have acted as easy-to-read barometers for the health and level of the lake. In the mid-1950s, for instance, the lake level fell so far that it was a long hike from the pier to the pleasure boats. Enterprising boatmen hired horse-drawn wagons to ferry tourists to their boats; later, a narrow channel was excavated to enable the boats to moor at the foot of the pier. Within little over a decade, the lake was full to overflowing; in 1967 it not only covered the pier but flooded downtown streets.

Chapala pier, 1967. (J. González)

Two major islands are visible from the jetty: Isla de los Alacranes (Scorpion Island) and Isla de Mezcala (Mezcala Island). The latter is sometimes called Isla del Presidio for its key role in Mexico's War of Independence and its famous ruins of a nineteenth century prison.

At the start of the twentieth century, when it became obvious from the success of the Hotel Arzapalo that Chapala had a bright future for tourism, all manner of tourist-related schemes were considered for these islands.

Isla de los Alacranes (Scorpion Island)

The island nearest to the pier was called Isla de Chapala prior to the end of the nineteenth century when it became known as Isla de Alacranes (Scorpion Island), presumably on account of the number of scorpions then inhabiting its rocky terrain.

The indigenous Huichol people have always known the island as Xapawiyemeta. It is one of their revered sites, the southernmost point of their sacred cosmos.[10]

Indigenous beliefs were certainly not taken into account when tourism started to transform Chapala. *The Mexican Herald* reported in 1896 that Isla de Alacranes, "a long thin insect-like bit of naked land reeking with alacranes" had been bought from the federal government by Mr. Pérez Verdía (presumed to be Luis Pérez Verdía) for "the nominal sum of twenty-one dollars." Pérez Verdía planned, after paying a bounty on dead scorpions, "to convert the Isla into a pleasure resort like Coney island."[11] He sold the island in about 1901 to Ernesto Paulsen, who intended to turn it into a "general sporting resort."[12]

Paulsen formed a company in Guadalajara in 1904 to establish an "American Monte Carlo" on the island, by constructing a modern 150-room hotel there with dancing pavilions, a bowling alley and a casino for roulette and poker. The company vice president was José María Schnaider and their partners included Aurelio González Hermosillo and Julio Lewels.[13]

The group renamed the island Isla Enriqueta. An "elegant sketch, in colors, of the plans," drawn by Guillermo de Alba, was exhibited at "La Palma," Behn & Paulsen's department store in Guadalajara. A few weeks later, the store added a "beautiful sketch in colors," drawn by Guadalajara architect Charles L. Strange, of the proposed hotel.[14]

These plans were never realized and three years later Paulsen sold the island to Arturo Braniff for $25,000.[15] Braniff announced his own big scheme for Isla de los Alacránes as it once again became known. He planned to enhance its natural beauty and "expend more than $150,000 in making it the finest summer home in Mexico."[16] His plans, too, ultimately came to nothing. After the Revolution, all private claims to the islands in the lake were revoked.

Isla de los Alacranes is still recognized by the Huichol people as a sacred site; they have undertaken annual pilgrimages to the island for generations to lay offerings in memory of their ancestors. Huichol leaders petitioned the state government in 2016 to grant their sacred ritual site formal protection against any and all future development.[17]

Mezcala Island (Isla del Presidio)

Mezcala Island, visible in the distance from the pier, is much larger than Isla de los Alacranes. Its nineteenth century history as an insurgent stronghold during Mexico's War of Independence, and then as a state jail, is well documented, and gave rise to its alternative name, Isla del Presidio.[18]

Like its smaller cousin, Mezcala Island was eyed by greedy developers as a viable location for a tourist hotel. For example, in 1904, Nicolas Tortolero y Vallejo, "a well-known young attorney of Guadalajara", asked the federal government to grant him full title to the island in exchange for ninety cents an acre, in order to build a lake resort there.[19] His offer was rejected.

The island features in two important Chapala-related novels. Much of the action in American author Charles Embree's landmark novel, *A Dream of a Throne,* published in 1900, takes place on Mezcala Island.[20] Two decades later, the English novelist D. H. Lawrence incorporated a thumbnail account of the island's historical importance as he described Kate's boat ride from Orilla to Sayula (Chapala) in *The Plumed Serpent.*[21]

The older structures on the island have been restored and stabilized, allowing present-day visitors to wander along nineteenth century cobblestone paths, between crumbling stone walls and through ancient doorways, as they marvel at the island's extraordinary history.

Chacaltita

The section of lakeshore east of the pier, towards the Chapala Yacht Club and the restaurant zone called Acapulquito, was a beach traditionally known as Chacaltita. Boats were built and repaired here and this is where Lawrence handwrote the first draft of *The Plumed Serpent* while sitting looking out at the lake from under the shade of a large tree.

Today, this area—with its park, playground, and small booths— would be totally unrecognizable to Lawrence. In his time, only a narrow beach separated the properties on the northern side of Paseo Ramón Corona from the lake. These houses lost their beachfront appeal at the end of the 1940s when the main jetty was extended and central Chapala was remodeled to create Paseo Ramón Corona. Not long after, many streets in central Chapala were paved for the first time. Quite rightly, architect Juan Palomar has publicly lamented the replacement of the ancient cobblestones with asphalt, writing that it destroyed the streets' traditional character and charm in "a misguided drive to modernity."[22]

The lakeshore park is on land reclaimed from the lake. Much of the material was obtained when the lake was dredged to improve navigation. The two-kilometer stretch of shoreline between the pier and the railroad station was also infilled with sediment; a large portion of this reclaimed land subsequently became Parque de la Cristiania.[23]

On a positive note, the creation of Paseo Ramón Corona now allows several of its noteworthy properties to be readily admired from the sidewalk.

Casa Braniff, c. 1907. (Photo by José María Lupercio?
Pub: Manuel Hernández / Schwidernoch, Austria)

36

Casa Braniff

While this iconic landmark right in the heart of Chapala, at Paseo Ramon Corona 18, is commonly called Casa Braniff (after the family that lived there for many years), it was originally built by influential Guadalajara lawyer and historian Luis Pérez Verdía. Construction of this magnificent edifice began in 1904 on the site of the first friary in Chapala. By the end of the nineteenth century, the friary buildings had fallen into disrepair and were used by the Hotel Arzapalo only as stables for the teams of horses that pulled their stagecoaches.

To design his new home, Pérez Verdía commissioned British architect George Edward King, who had previously built Villa Tlalocan for the British consul, Lionel Carden.

Pérez Verdía, born in 1857, grew up in the intellectual milieu of Guadalajara and was a member of the Ateneo Jalisciense, Jalisco's leading artistic-scientific society. The society, active at the very start of the twentieth century, brought together a host of distinguished writers, artists and musicians, including photographer José María Lupercio, violinist and painter Félix Bernardelli, and artist and author Gerardo Murillo (Dr. Atl).[1]

Pérez Verdía had been the official representative for Jalisco at the 11th International Americanistas Congress in Mexico City in 1895, an event also attended by Cora Townsend and her mother, Mary Ashley Townsend (Cora bought Villa Montecarlo as her mother's Christmas present that year!), and British consul Carden, who had already begun building Villa Tlalocan.[2]

Besides working as a lawyer, and later as a magistrate and state congressman, Pérez Verdía founded Jalisco's college for teachers (Escuela

Normal). He took up a diplomatic post as Minister of Mexico in 1913 in Guatemala, where he died the following year.

Contemporary accounts paint Pérez Verdía as the archetypal man of high status in Porfirian times: strict, impeccably attired, methodical, religious and extremely well-mannered, but always guarding his privacy except in the company of immediate family. His one vanity was an enormous handlebar moustache.[3]

Construction of Pérez Verdía's house began in 1904. Expected to cost $30,000, the "fine residence" was to be "a modern structure in every way."[4] By June, with work well underway, the estimated cost of the house had already risen to $40,000.[6]

Contrary to later conjecture, the bricks for Pérez Verdía's house were not imported from Europe; *The Jalisco Times* reported that:

> as soon as a supply of fuel arrives at King's station, on the Central, the big brickyards there will fire up and get the machinery in operation. The output will be shipped to Guadalajara and this place.[5]

Architect George Edward King and his son (also an architect) spent several days in Chapala that August overseeing work on the house.[7] When it was completed early the following year (1905), the state government agreed to exempt the property from all municipal and state taxes for a period of ten years.[8]

This generosity did not make Pérez Verdía any more benevolent towards the local council when it complained to state authorities that the garden of his house occupied federal property and prevented the smooth flow of people along the only beachfront promenade in town. The group that visited him to express their concern was received with extreme cordiality, but it was more than a year before Pérez Verdía finally agreed to concede the land in question.[9]

The quixotic design of the house was perfectly encapsulated in words by American poet Witter Bynner, who first saw it in 1923 when walking from the house rented by D. H. Lawrence to the Hotel Arzapalo:

> We came by a pretentious Victorian brick villa, in the convulsive style of architecture—bay windows, turrets, cupolas, stained-glass windows.[10]

Alberto Braniff, a wealthy Mexico City businessman, bought Pérez Verdía's house and all its furnishings in 1907 for "$57,000 cash," as a gift for his mother, who had lost her husband two years earlier. Two of Alberto's older brothers also invested in Lake Chapala at this time. Arturo, who kept a fast launch at the Rivera Castellanos resort near Ocotlán, bought Scorpion Island. Thomás was reported to have "purchased considerable land in San Juan, a small place on the lake some distance west of the town of Chapala."[11]

The patriarch of the Braniff family was Irish-American Thomas Braniff (1830–1905), who had left New York for Mexico in 1863 to work on the Mexico City-Veracruz railroad. An astute businessman, he eventually became the railroad's director. His wife, Lorenza Ricard (1847–1932), was French and had strong business connections to the enterprising Barcelonette community from southern France that became highly influential in Guadalajara business circles. The Braniff family's Mexico City residence was a 34-room mansion with ballroom on Paseo de la Reforma, and they were close confidantes of President Díaz, who was Alberto Braniff's godfather.

The Braniff brothers loved dangerous pursuits and owned a succession of imported racing cars and speed boats. Alberto Braniff (1885–1966) made the first successful aircraft flight in Latin America. Braniff took off from the family's Hacienda Balbuena, close to Mexico's City's present-day international airport, in his imported Voissin biplane on 8 January 1910, and flew 500 meters at a maximum height of 25 meters.[12] Barely three weeks later, he was in Mexico's first airplane accident when he crashed his plane, fortunately without any casualties or serious injuries.[13]

Alberto spent at least a month each year at Chapala and liked to arrange bull fights during his stay. Guadalajara writer Ixca Farías, a regular visitor to Chapala in those early days, later recalled how, in about 1908, Braniff had rented hundreds and hundreds of wooden boards to erect a temporary bullring, and brought in fighting bulls from distant haciendas. In addition to Braniff, Luis Pérez Verdía also entered the ring to test his prowess as a matador against the stressed and angry animals that had been brought from Ocotlán in individual crates on large *canoas*.[14]

Casa Braniff remained in the Braniff family until 1942 when it was bought by Zenen Camarena, acting on behalf of Camarena and Concuera, S.A. For a short time, the house was named Chalet Camarena, which may explain why it is still occasionally claimed that the house once belonged to Duncan Cameron, the Scotsman who introduced steamboats to Mexico in the 1860s, despite the fact that Cameron died in 1903, the year it was bought by Alberto Braniff.

Casa Braniff then passed through several hands before being acquired in 1970 by José Luis Martínez Covarrubias and several partners, who converted it into a restaurant.[15] Patrons of the Cazadores Casa Braniff today can still admire some of the original silk tapestry wall coverings, beautiful stained-glass windows and period features and antiques that adorn this remarkable historic building.[16]

Villa Robles León, 2016.

37

Villa Robles León

Readily identifiable by its highly distinctive rounded sides, Villa Robles León (Paseo Ramón Corona 14) has been vacant for years and is in an exceptionally sad state of neglect, despite its close links to Luis Barragán.

Photos from the 1920s show that Villa Robles León (precise age unclear) was originally a two-story structure with a wrap-around ground floor columned veranda. The floor above had a balcony, accessed from the interior via a door facing the lake. Oval windows either side of the door completed the symmetry of the upper story facade.[1]

Villa Robles León was remodeled in the 1930s by Barragán and Ignacio Díaz Morales for Emiliano Robles León (1888–1961), a notable lawyer, notary and academic whose clients included Barragán's father. When Luis Barragán, then aged 25, returned in 1927 from his first trip to Europe, Robles León commissioned him to remodel the interior spaces of his Guadalajara home. Barragán's success was evident and a few years later, by which time Díaz Morales was working with him, he was asked to redesign the lawyer's vacation home in Chapala.

Barragán and Díaz Morales, fellow graduates of the Escuela Libre de Ingenieros in Guadalajara,[2] were greatly influenced by the modernist style of French architect Ferdinand Bac. The happy combination of modernism and local architectural creativity, as evidenced by these and other talented architects, gave rise to the Tapatío school of architecture. Another member of this group, Pedro Castellanos (architect of Villa Ferrara) worked on two of the buildings between Casa Braniff and Villa Robles León.[3]

At Villa Robles León, Barragán added a third story to create the equivalent of a master bedroom (with its own bathroom) on the top level. Communal spaces were on the ground floor, below four bedrooms on the second floor. Díaz Morales (1905–1992), whose teaching at the University of Guadalajara's School of Architecture influenced several later generations of architects, designed the size, position and style of the window openings to allow natural light to enter the home and play across the interiors, giving ever-changing effects of light and shadow throughout the day. To the rear, the property had an extensive orchard and garden.

From the street, unlike most homes in Chapala, the arched entranceway to the property is positioned off-center at one extremity of its southern boundary wall, a wall made of long, thin bricks arranged as a series of "V"s forming a geometric wave design. Several aspects of the home's design were apparently inspired by a boat.[4] Like all the other old properties along the north side of Paseo Ramón Corona, Villa Robles León used to look directly onto the beach and the lake.

The house was apparently used regularly in later life by José Guadalupe Zuno Hernández (1891–1980), who had been the Governor of Jalisco from 1923 to 1926. Zuno was a staunch and outspoken defender of the lake during its crisis years in the drought of the 1950s.[5]

Villa Carmen, c. 1907. (Photo by José María Lupercio? Pub: Manuel Hernández)

38

Villa Carmen

Villa Carmen, a prominent landmark on early photographs of Chapala, stood on the large corner lakefront property at Paseo Ramón Corona 13, bounded on the east by Calle Zaragoza. Tiles on its boundary wall show it once had an address of Zaragoza 302. This property changed names and owners several times over the years.

The original Villa Carmen, the work of an unidentified architect, was a two-story home erected at the end of the nineteenth century and long-since demolished. Property titles show it was owned in 1899 by Manuela Castillo Negrete de Mora. According to contemporary newspapers, it was built by her husband, Roberto de la Mora, and definitely finished and occupied prior to December 1898,[1] some months ahead of Villa Ochoa, located slightly further to the east. The de la Moras, both born in 1863, were members of a numerous, intermarried and prominent Guadalajara family.

The eight-room home occupied a 246-square-meter plot bought from Antonio Barba in 1896; its estimated value in 1899 was 2500 pesos.[2] Mrs. Manuela Castillo Negrete de Mora also bought two other large, adjoining pieces of land—one from Antonio Barba[3] in November 1896, and one from Ramona Sánchez in 1898—to extend her estate northwards, giving her the space to plant an extensive orchard.

Roberto de la Mora died at some point prior to 1922.[4] Following Manuela's death, the Villa Carmen property was transferred in May 1926 to Fernando Puga, a lawyer who co-owned the house with his wife, Margarita Ortiz de Puga, and renamed it Villa Margarita. In 1934 they sold the property (now a total area of 4455 square meters) to Refugio Martín del Campo de Robles León.[5] The original Villa Carmen was also briefly known as Villa Sergio before eventually being pulled down and replaced.

Like its neighbors, this property lost its direct access to the beach when Paseo Ramón Corona was created.

———————— • •●• • ————————

Casa de las Cuentas (D.H. Lawrence house), c. 1954. Photo by Roy MacNicol. By this time the half-moon entrance, designed by Luis Barragán a decade earlier, no longer had its original heavy wooden gates.

39

Casa de las Cuentas (the D. H. Lawrence house)

In the first block north on Calle Zaragoza is the house that English author D. H. Lawrence rented in 1923. The original name for this street was Calle de la Pesquería ("Fishing street") because this is where local fishermen repaired their nets and hung them out to dry.

The Lawrence house, at Zaragoza 307, is thought to date back to the nineteenth century and is where the great novelist wrote the first draft of *The Plumed Serpent*. Lawrence and his wife, Frieda, rented the house—then only a single-story dwelling—from the start of May 1923 until early July.

Lawrence had been in Mexico City when he read about Chapala in *Terry's Guide to Mexico* and decided to catch the next train to Guadalajara and explore the lakeside village for himself. He clearly liked what he saw. Within hours of arrival, he sent an urgent telegram back to his wife and traveling companions in the capital, pronouncing Chapala "paradise" and urging the others to join him there immediately.

Lawrence christened the house Casa de las Cuentas ("House of the Beads"), after the tree shading one corner of the property.[1] The seeds of the tree can be strung together to make rosaries. The British novelist's delight at the luxuriant beauty of his surroundings is evident in his description (based on this house) of Kate's living quarters in *The Plumed Serpent*:

> Her house was what she wanted; a low, L-shaped, tiled building with rough red floors and deep veranda, and the other two sides of the patio completed by the thick, dark little mango forest outside the low wall. The square of the patio, within the precincts of the house and the mango trees, was gay with oleanders and hibiscus, and there was

a basin of water in the seedy grass. The flowerpots along the veranda were full of flowering geranium and foreign flowers.[2]

In subsequent decades, the house was extensively remodeled more than once and acquired links to several other famous writers and artists in the process.

The major alterations carried out by famed architect Luis Barragán in 1940, for then owner Gustavo Cristo, were described and illustrated the following year in *House and Garden*.[3] Barragán designed a striking "half-moon entrance gateway, with heavy wooden grill work painted red outside and French blue inside" that added an Oriental touch, characteristic of much of his work of this period. Inside, Barragán "had the sandstone flagging of the porch carried on into the sala without a break, so that the house and terrace merge into each other." He also designed a spectacular rounded bay window for the dining room, with built-in steel shelves for a collection of hand-blown blue, gold and amethyst-colored glass.[4]

American artist and architect Roy MacNicol, who acquired the house in 1954, added a swimming pool. He also placed a memorial ceramic plaque on the exterior wall stating: "In this house D. H. Lawrence lived and wrote 'The Plumed Serpent' in the year 1923."[5]

MacNicol (1889–1970), known as the "Paintbrush Ambassador," led an extraordinarily colorful life, in the course of which he married at least four times and was the focus of numerous scandals and lawsuits. He first visited Mexico in the 1940s and is credited with creating the first Good Neighbor Exhibition, which was Mexican themed and promoted international goodwill. Later Good Neighbor exhibits were sponsored by Eleanor Roosevelt, and by prominent Mexican officials, including President Miguel Alemán.[6]

While living here, MacNicol's then wife, Mary, became so engrossed in local cuisine, especially that involving flowers, that she wrote an entire book of flower-based recipes, including one called "Chapala Cheer":

> Wash 10-12 squash blossoms and remove stems. Drain dry on paper towels. Mix other ingredients (2 eggs, beaten; 2-3 tablespoons water; flour; salt and pepper) to make a smooth batter. Dip blossoms in batter and fry in oil until brown. Serve hot.[7]

A second story had been added to the Lawrence house by the time Colonel Eddie Laborde and his wife, Helen, bought it in the 1960s.

Laborde, a famed aviator, had served in both world wars, making friends with flying greats ranging from Eddie Rickenbacker and Harold "Hap Arnold" to Amelia Earhart and Charles Lindberg.[8] He was awarded the Aztec Eagle, Mexico's highest honor for foreigners, for his contributions to promoting civilian flights. The Labordes sold the house in 1968 to move to Guadalajara.

In the late 1970s the house was the subject of a limited edition book. Canadian poet Al Purdy, a great admirer of Lawrence—to the point of having a bust of Lawrence on the hall table at his home in Ontario—wrote *The D. H. Lawrence House at Chapala*, based on a poem about his great hero.[9]

In 1978 the Lawrence house was acquired by a Californian couple, Dick and Barbi Henderson, who remodeled it to accommodate friends visiting from the US. After buying the adjoining lot in 1982 to add two additional units and extend the gardens, they ran the property as Quinta Quetzalcoatl, a boutique bed and breakfast with eight luxury suites.[10]

Under a series of different owners, Quinta Quetzalcoatl has remained an exclusive boutique hotel ever since.

Villa Ochoa, 2016.

40

Villa Ochoa

Several buildings on Paseo Ramón Corona between Calle Zaragoza and Calle 5 de Mayo have architectural significance.[1] Paseo Ramón Corona 11 was designed by Pedro Castellanos Lambley and dates from the 1930s. Number 10 is an earlier dwelling, thought, like the Lawrence house, to have been owned by Gustavo Cristo and completely transformed by Luis Barragán at the end of the 1930s. The next-door property (number 9) is believed to be the work of engineer Aurelio Aceves.[2]

However, by far the most interesting and important of the buildings at this end of Paseo Ramón Corona is the two-story Villa Ochoa (Paseo Ramón Corona 6).

Villa Ochoa, somewhat astonishingly, and unlike almost all the other old villas in Chapala, is still owned by direct descendants of Carlos Ochoa Arroniz (1847–1943), the tall, blue-eyed and personable civil engineer who built it as his family's vacation home. In an unusual departure from the norm for the time, the entire second floor was reserved exclusively for the engineer's private studio, while the ground floor had all the dwelling's living quarters and communal spaces.[3]

Ochoa, who had studied at the College of Mining in Mexico City, was the government engineer appointed to make improvements to the Santiago river at the end of the nineteenth century, at a time when it was believed that moving cargo by water was the key to building an efficient transportation system for this region of Mexico.

Prior to the advent of efficient roads, water-borne vessels could easily out-compete land-based vehicles for transporting people and goods around and across the lake. Successive state administrations hoped to increase the area having efficient transport by making more use of the

Rivers Lerma and Santiago, which meant improving key stretches to make them navigable by larger boats.

Ochoa also helped build the Mexico City-Veracruz railroad and worked on several railroads in western Mexico.[4] It was while he was working for the Atequiza hacienda that he discovered Chapala and decided it was the ideal place for a holiday home.[5]

Early in 1898, Villa Ochoa was still "nearing completion."[6] While this date does not fit with the tiles dated 1885 on the building's terrace,[7] perhaps the tiles came from an earlier building or commemorated some other family event.

After Ochoa's death in 1943, Villa Ochoa was passed down in the family. A decade ago, it came into the capable hands of a great-grandson, architect Jaime Troop Ochoa, who has restored this epoch-defining building and its collection of period furnishings to something like their former grandeur.[8]

Chapala pier and Yacht Club, c. 1915. (Anon)

41

Chapala Yacht Club

The clubhouse and grounds of Chapala Yacht Club (Paseo Ramón Corona 1), normally open only to members or invited guests, are occasionally used for public events and exhibitions. The largest annual event here is Feria Maestros del Arte, founded by Mexican folk art expert Marianne Carlson in the early 2000s. Now one of Mexico's most important annual exhibitions of folk art, it showcases the highly creative work of dozens of indigenous artisans from all over the country.

The Chapala Yacht Club has a lengthy history. As described earlier, after several failed early attempts to start a club, Schjetnan and his partners had succeeded in opening one in 1911, only for the installations to be accidentally burned down a few years later.

The first sailing and rowing regattas had been held during Holy Week in 1908 with President Díaz in attendance. Díaz watched two local young ladies (Lupe Capetillo and Gabriella Saldaña Galván) triumph in the female pairs rowing competition; festivities concluded with a party and fireworks.[1]

Events at an aquatic festival in the 1930s included a swimming race from Scorpion Island to Chapala, a motorboat race from El Manglar to Chapala, and a regata for rowboats on a course from the Villa Montecarlo to the town pier.[2]

A two-day international powerboat regatta was held on Lake Chapala in November 1947, in which thirty American craft and nine Mexican boats competed for the Copa Jalisco, a 10-kilo silver cup donated by the then state governor, J. Jesús González Gallo.[3]

The current Chapala Yacht Club dates back to a meeting held at Villa Montecarlo in 1958,[4] immediately after the lake level began to climb back to normal for the first time in a decade. The Yacht Club had attracted

100 members by 1959; within ten years, it had double that number.[5] The official inauguration of the club was held in 1960.

Club regattas, complete with a big annual ball, were held each September, timed to coincide with Mexico's annual Independence celebrations. Members in the 1960s included Eduardo Collignon, who owned the ocean-going racing yacht "Capricho", in which he competed in the four-day Manzanillo-Acapulco race each year.

In March 1961 the Chapala Yacht Club organized Mexico's Second Interclub Regatta[6] and the following year it co-organized (with the Guadalajara Club de Regatas) an International Regatta, which attracted more than 65 entries from all over Mexico.[7] Chapala Yacht Club has hosted the National Regatta several times, including 1963 (the Third National Regatta) and 1965.[8]

The clubhouse was designed by Federico González Gortázar. Inside is a mural entitled "The Holy Virgin helps and protects the navigators of this your lake," painted by José María de Servín.

Over the years, the clubhouse and beautifully landscaped grounds have witnessed hundreds of art exhibits, book presentations, fund-raising events, celebrations and parties.

Former Railroad Station, now Centro Cultural González Gallo, 2020.

42

Chapala Railroad Station

Four blocks along Avenida González Gallo from the Red Cross station (across from the Chapala Yacht Club) is the elegant and imposing former Chapala Railroad Station, now the Centro Cultural González Gallo.

Traveling from Guadalajara to Chapala in the mid-nineteenth century, whether on horseback or by stagecoach (*diligencia*), was an arduous journey taking twelve hours or more, depending on the season and the road conditions. The trip required a change of horses mid-way, which often necessitated an overnight stop. Relatively few people braved all the uncertainties (and the bandits regularly encountered outside the large cities) to visit Chapala or Ajijic.

The expansion of Mexico's railroad network was the key to Lake Chapala becoming a tourism destination in the final years of the nineteenth century.

As railroad mania spread across Mexico, wealthy Tapatíos, many of whom had agricultural or other interests at Lake Chapala, saw the potential for a railroad connecting Guadalajara to the lake. The idea was first seriously proposed in the 1860s by the Compañía de Navegación del Lago de Chapala y Río Grande (Lake Chapala Navigation Company),[1] which ran a passenger sternwheeler on the lake, but the company's plan for a railroad fizzled out.

Access to Lake Chapala from Mexico City and central Mexico was dramatically improved when the Mexican Central Railroad (Ferrocarril Central Mexicano)—which linked Mexico City to Ciudad Juárez—opened its branch line from Irapuato to Guadalajara via the town of Ocotlán in 1888.[2] Ocotlán, situated on the River Santiago (which flows from Lake Chapala towards Guadalajara), was only a few kilometers from the lake. Passengers could disembark at Ocotlán from their train, walk or take a short tram ride to the wharves on the banks of the river Zula, near its confluence with the Santiago, and then board a boat to take them to Lake Chapala.

This meant it was now possible to make a day trip from Guadalajara to Chapala by taking the train as far as Ocotlán to connect with the steamer that left Ocotlán at about 9.00am and returned at 4.00pm. The alternative was to stay on the train only as far as Atequiza, and then take a horse or stagecoach on to Chapala. Either way, it became much easier for Tapatíos to visit Chapala and explore the lake.

The Mexican Central Railroad, realizing the tourism potential, commissioned American writer Thomas L. Rogers to visit Mexico in July 1892 and write a travelogue of all the places and regions that its ever-expanding network was opening up for travelers.[3] These included the impressive Juanacatlán Falls, the "Niagara of Mexico", mid-way between Guadalajara and Atequiza.

Wealthy Tapatíos still yearned for a more direct link between their city and Chapala, especially now that an increasing number of them possessed elegant second homes there. A number of early proposals for a Guadalajara–Chapala railroad—including a regular gauge line in 1882, a narrow-gauge Decauville system in 1891 (and again in 1900)[4] and an electric train in 1902—were all frustrated by a lack of investors.

It dawned on a later group of wealthy landowners, chaired by local politician Luciano Gallardo, in 1910 that it would be simpler and less costly to start any new rail line to Chapala not from Guadalajara but from Atequiza station, which was very much closer to the lake.[5] Even these plans were shelved within months when Díaz and his cronies were forced out of office, taking with them any immediate hope of federal financing.

It was this 1910 project—to build a railroad from the mainline at Atequiza to Chapala, with a series of small stations along the way and a terminus in Chapala—that was taken up by the visionary Norwegian entrepreneur Christian Schjetnan.

Ever the optimist, Schjetnan was not planning to build only a railroad and a few simple stations. He envisaged a luxurious and grand station terminal hotel in Chapala as the focal point for a magnificent park and scores of beautiful residences. It was an unbelievably ambitious idea. It is impossible to imagine the headaches and heartaches that Schjetnan endured over the next decade. Between 1911 and 1920 (when the railroad finally opened), Schjetnan had to deal with no fewer than a dozen different individuals who occupied the position of state governor. It was equally complicated at the federal level, with some periods when it was difficult to know who was in charge.

When he first became involved with this project, Schjetnan had absolutely no idea how long the political unrest in Mexico might last, making his decision to proceed with such a grandiose scheme, despite the obvious challenges, even more remarkable.

The Hotel Plaza and Chapala Development Company

Schjetnan wasted no time in planning the first phase of his railroad project. Mexico's National Water History Archive (Archivo Histórico del Agua) has an architect's drawing, dated 1912, of his proposed Hotel Plaza and railroad station, to be constructed on the lakeshore.[6] The drawing does not appear to be the work of Guillermo de Alba, who was later commissioned to design the Chapala Railroad Station, but may be the work of noted Norwegian-American architect Arne Dehli (1857–1942), who was, in 1920, announced as the chosen architect for the luxury hotel.[7] Born in Norway, Dehli trained in Germany before moving to New York, where he designed churches, the nurses' home for the Norwegian Hospital, various business structures and the zoological building in Prospect Park, Brooklyn.[8] Sadly, plans for the hotel never made it beyond the drawing board.

The big problem, as always, was funding. Promises of federal funding given while President Díaz was still in office became worthless after he was deposed. Schjetnan turned to the Jalisco state government and negotiated a contract in 1911 in which he promised to find $200,000 from private investors, provided the state would guarantee them an annual return of 6% once the line was built.

When the state withdrew its financial backing two years later,[9] Schjetnan returned to his native Norway to seek new investors. According to a Norwegian account, Schjetnan showed prospective investors

> a concession document from Mexico, issued by Carranza's Government on 13 November 1915, for the construction and operation of a railroad from La Capilla to the town of Chapala, with the right to purchase 400,000 square meters of land.

Among other things, the prospectus claimed that one of the railroad's "elegant railroad cars" would have "its own compartment for Negroes."[10]

Schjetnan was an extremely persuasive individual. His sales pitches extolled the undoubted virtues of the railroad and emphasized that building a first class hotel would help turn Chapala into Mexico's largest tourist and health resort. In addition, an embankment along the lakeshore would protect 200,000 square meters of land that could be developed for private villas, while a combined yacht and automotive club with casino would further boost future revenues. Schjetnan's master plan, in short, would create "an El Dorado for the country's richest, a sought-after place for the country's jeunesse dorée."[11] Norwegians were sufficiently entranced with Schjetnan's dreams for this remote lake on the other side of the world that they happily parted with "hundreds of thousands of Norwegian kroner," at a time when there were 3.5 kroner to a dollar.

Unfortunately for these investors, Mexico was, during the Revolution, a risky place in which to do business. Ultimately, according to this Norwegian account, investors lost their shirts; the only "dividends" they ever received were a few worthless photos of locomotives and rolling stock.[12]

Schjetnan, however, had finally acquired some much-needed operating capital, and his luck began to change. Mexico's new federal constitution in 1917 brought greater safeguards for investors. Within days of the new constitution being approved, Schjetnan formed the Compañía de Fomento de Chapala, S.A. (Chapala Development Company).[13] In addition to Schjetnan, the shareholders included Eugenio Pinzón, Antonio L. Ruíz, Aurelio González Hermosillo, Jesús Camarena and Manuel P. Chávez. The company had a share capital of $550,000, with Schjetnan, as company president, holding almost all of the 5500 shares.

By mid-March 1917, Schjetnan—claiming to represent various Norwegian syndicates and boasting that the company now had working capital of $800,000.00 *"oro nacional"* with guarantees of more—had signed a contract with the Jalisco state government to build a railroad from La Capilla to Chapala. The Guadalajara daily *El Informador* reported that all the capital came from Norway.[14]

The Chapala Railroad

Schjetnan contracted a young Norwegian engineer, Birger Winsnes,[15] to join him in Mexico and be his chief engineer, assisted by Guadalajara engineer Juan José Barragán, the brother of modernist architect Luis Barragán.

With survey work completed, the final route chosen for the railroad began at La Capilla on the mainline, rather than at Atequiza. From La Capilla the Chapala Railroad track ran alongside the main line before branching off to Hacienda Buenavista and Ixtlahuacán de los Membrillos. It then went across the hills, via Arroyo de los Sabinos, Cerro del Chihue, and Potrero del Molino to Santa Cruz de la Soledad, before the final stretch along the lake shore to the outskirts of Chapala. The total length of this route was 26.3 kilometers (16.2 miles).[16]

Hundreds of workers were hired to dig ditches, build embankments and start laying track. All the specialist materials and equipment needed had to be imported from the US via the port of San Blas. Progress was slow and each rainy season threatened to derail the project when it washed out work completed earlier in the year.

In 1918, Schjetnan asked the state government to sell him 350 hectares of land in Chapala for the railroad station and other buildings.[17] By the end of that year, railroad work was well underway: the first sections of rails had been laid and Winsnes was supervising 100 men putting in the foundations for the Chapala station, designed by Guillermo de Alba.[18] It was to be the final building de Alba designed and, in many ways, the crowning glory of his architectural career.

In 1919, with the railroad almost complete, the Chapala Development Company launched a passenger steamship service on the lake by purchasing and remodeling an abandoned ship into the double-decked *Viking*, which could carry 200 passengers.[19] The company ran a second steamer, the *Tapatía*, for freight, to transport fruit and other produce to villages around the lake. Schjetnan, who had decided to add a yachting area to the master plan, was offering to help people purchase various kinds of boats.[20]

By the end of the year everything seemed to be finally falling into place for the grand opening of the Chapala Railroad Station.

Schjetnan was on the verge of success, but the multiple delays meant that his company's cash reserves were critically depleted. The company had given the state government $25,000 pesos in gold as a deposit, repayable when work was complete, and Schjetnan now asked for it to be repaid. The state refused, though, arguing that the company had failed to meet its agreed deadlines, a decision later upheld in court.

The official inauguration of the Chapala Railroad and the Chapala Railroad Station took place on Thursday 8 April 1920.[21] An eight-car train was given a rousing send-off from Guadalajara at about 9.00am to

Birger Winsnes

Birger Winsnes (1890-1969) was born in Kristiania (Oslo), Norway, on 2 July 1890. The 5' 10" tall, blue-eyed Winsnes arrived in Mexico in 1917 to work as the chief engineer for the Chapala Railroad. His work included several trips to the US to oversee the purchase of equipment.

Winsnes was invited in 1917 to the traditional Christmas dinner given annually at Hacienda Buenavista by its owner Manuel Capetillo Quevedo.[22] Two of Capetillo's daughters—Lupe and María Elena—were also in attendance, and this is probably when the young engineer first met María Elena, his future bride. Four years later, Carlos Ochoa Arroniz (Villa Ochoa), Guillermo de Alba (Mi Pullman), Eugenio Pinzón and Alf Ericcsen were witnesses to their marriage, held at the family hacienda.

In May 1940, Winsnes and Agustín Farías (who had the concession for bathing huts on the beach in front of the Hotel Arzapalo in 1922) helped resolve an attempt to expropriate land in Chapala still owned by Christian Schjetnan.[23] The Club Deportivo de Chapala (led by Luis Cuevas Pimienta and Manuel Carrillo) wanted to use the property and asked for it to be expropriated. Winsnes and Farías successfully negotiated an agreement by which the club paid one peso a year for the use of the property while respecting Schjetnan's right of ownership.[24]

On 10 November 1944, Winsnes was awarded a federal concession for the industrial exploitation of the water hyacinth (*lirio*) in the River Santiago, and its tributaries, as well as at Poncitlán, El Salto, and other places.[25] Under the terms of the five-year contract, Winsnes had to install a factory to process it, and to invest $10,000 pesos within the first year. The contract allowed for extensions, subject to the terms being met. It is unclear whether or not this venture was successful.

Winsnes served as the honorary vice-consul for Norway in Guadalajara from 15 September 1924 until his death in the city on 15 May 1969.

the sound of a brass band, train whistles and applause. President Carranza had made his excuses at the last minute, and the state governor, perhaps because of the rancor over the return of the deposit, was also a no-show. Their absence, however, did nothing to dampen the general enthusiasm or the celebrations.

Most of the 250 distinguished guests were members of *Tapatío* high society.[26] Fashionably attired in blue blazers and bow ties or elegant frocks (with some of the younger set in racy dresses), they switched trains at La Capilla at about 10.30am in front of a crowd of 1000 cheering onlookers. The Chapala train was underway!

Greeted by curious onlookers at every station, the train pulled into the magnificent Chapala station in time for a quick tour of the building before lunch at the Hotel Palmera. After a leisurely lunch—including the local specialty, caldo michi—guests danced the afternoon away to a live orchestra, before catching the return train back to the big city shortly after 5.00pm.

Many of the visitors opted to remain in Chapala overnight, staying with friends or in one of the hotels. After a formal dinner that evening, followed by a mock battle with fireworks on *canoas* on the lake, Schjetnan threw a lavish private party for special guests that ran well into the following morning.[27]

Regular daily rail service began a few days later. Initially, the train made two daily trips each way, but this was later reduced to a single daily return trip. The Chapala Railroad had two locomotives (#25 and #26), three first-class passenger cars with plush red velvet seats, three second-class cars with plain wooden benches, and several extra wagons for baggage and freight.

In November 1920 the round-trip from Guadalajara for a Sunday excursion to the lake cost $5.00 pesos first class and $2.50 second class.[28] Chapala station had a restaurant on the ground floor where the set menu (*comida corrida*) cost $1.50.[29]

The railroad reduced the travel time between Guadalajara and Chapala from the five-plus hours by stagecoach to about three hours each way, bringing a tremendous surge of tourists to the lakeside town and its hotels. The political upheavals seemed to have come to an end. It looked like there were more settled times ahead and expectations ran high.

Work on Schjetnan's other projects was proceeding only slowly when Chapala mayor Miguel Martinez demanded to know, in 1922, whether Schjetnan's company had been limiting access to streets near "Avenida Cristiana" that had been built for public use.[30] This is one of the earliest references to the street running in front of the railroad station that is now known as either Avenida Cristianía or Avenida González Gallo. Another early reference to the street, also dating from 1922, spells it "Cristiania,"[31] which raises the interesting question as to whether the street was originally named Cristiana (presumably for Christian Schjetnan) or Cristianía (for Christiania, as Oslo, the capital of Norway, was still familiarly called).[32]

This street echoed to the footsteps of D. H. Lawrence and his friends at various times in 1923 during their stay in Chapala as they made their way to and from Guadalajara to shop or visit the Purnells. Witter Bynner, recalling the first time he accompanied Lawrence on the train, wrote how the novelist had explained that a Scandinavian had sold land, "not only to trusting Mexicans but to foreigners as well"... including, in Lawrence's words, "a whole moony cult from California." Bynner learned that, "because of far too much financial outlay at the start, the Scandinavian's scheme had collapsed and with it his title and the titles of his victims."[33]

Sadly for both Schjetnan and the town, the Chapala railroad never did become profitable, especially in the face of the increased competition from automobiles and buses for the passenger traffic between Guadalajara and Chapala.

The railroad was already struggling when exceptionally heavy rains swelled the lake on 27 August 1926 to the highest level ever recorded in the twentieth century.[34] The lake rose so high that it flooded the picturesque station, built right on the beach, to a height of more than a meter. The tracks disappeared from view; train service had to be suspended.

The company faced other problems, too. Later that same year (1926), its *Viking* passenger steamship was battered by storm waves and badly damaged. Then, in October, authorities closed the company's offices in Guadalajara due to labor complaints.[35] Days later, the Compañia de Fomento de Chapala sought a court injunction to prevent the confiscation of its property and goods. The Chapala–La Capilla Railroad closed down, its offices and stations were shuttered, and the town of Chapala was thrown back a decade.

A limited local service was provided for a short time by a Sr. Arciniega. He ran railroad coaches he had built himself along a short stretch of the existing track.[36]

Railroad Station restored as Cultural Center

The solidly-built station building in Chapala still stood, though legal complications prevented it from being given an alternative use. In 1940 the Compañia de Fomento de Chapala fought to prevent the repossession of the station.[37] Seven years later, in 1947, the courts seized and auctioned off 1400 square meters of company land to meet a $20,000 payout awarded to Birger Winsnes when he won a lawsuit against the company.[38] The Chapala Railroad Station was later acquired by Ricardo Aguilar (owner at one-time of the lakefront El Manglar estate), before being bought by J. Jesús González Gallo during his tenure as state governor.

In 1954 the building and surrounding grounds were leased for use as a golf clubhouse. The nine-hole course, which extended onto adjoining property (now the Parque de la Cristianía), was under water whenever the lake level was high. The golf club later built a new nine-hole course further east in Vista del Lago.

After González Gallo's untimely death in a motor vehicle accident in 1957, ownership of the station passed to his heirs. They allowed it to be used in 1964 by a theater group (the forerunner to the Lakeside Little Theater), whose first production, directed by Betty Kuzell, was George S. Kaufman's brilliant satire, *If Men Played Cards as Women Do.*[39]

As the building gradually fell into disrepair, it became a squat for as many as ten families (45 people) at a time. After González Gallo's family donated the building to the state in 1992, Jim Kaye and other members of the foreign community provided the families with simple new homes elsewhere on land donated by the city.

A committee, formed after the building passed into state ownership, succeeded in gaining support for its restoration through a grant from the federal Adopt a Work of Art program. Patricia Urzúa and Sandra Loridans, the State Regent of the Thomas Paine Chapter of the Daughters of the American Revolution, were prominent among the many active committee members and fund raisers. Restoration began in 1998.

By a stroke of good fortune, the original blueprints were unearthed at an early stage of the process and the restoration is fairly faithful to the original design. The building retains some original flooring and architectural details, though it was felt necessary to add tall glass panels to close in the formerly open station vestibule to protect it from the weather.

The former station reopened on 28 March 2006 as the Jesús González Gallo Cultural Center in a gala affair attended by Mexico's then first lady, Martha Sahagún de Fox, and Christian Schjetnan Garduño, a grandson of the pioneering Norwegian whose vision had helped create the landmark building.[40] The cultural center houses a small permanent collection of artifacts and is regularly used for temporary exhibits. It also displays examples of the works of two internationally-renowned artists: Mexican sculptor Miguel Miramontes (1918–2015), who had his studio in Chapala for decades, and Austrian-born painter Georg Rauch (1924–2006), who lived and painted in Jocotepec for thirty years.

The closing of the railroad station brought to an end a marvelous chapter in the dreams of the early twentieth-century entrepreneurs and pioneers who raised the sleepy town of Chapala to national prominence. Their efforts initiated the influx of foreign residents which has continued to the present day. It is entirely fitting that the truly splendid historic building in Chapala that was once the Chapala Railroad Station is now the González Gallo Cultural Center.

●

Notes

Endnotes marked * refer to text in boxes

Introduction. Chapala's Rise to International Prominence

1. Thomas L. Rogers, *Mexico? Sí, señor,* 157-158.
2. Gibbon, *Guadalajara (La Florencia Mexicana),* 316.
3. No definitive evidence has yet been found for this assertion, made in various Spanish-language accounts.
4. F.R.G., "From Chapala," *The Mexican Herald,* 15 March 1898, 4.
5. Ibid.
6. Palomar Verea, 2016, "La ciudad y los días," *El Informador,* 3 August 2016.
7. AHMC, unpublished time line, entry for 1889.
8. AHMC, unpublished time line, entry for 1910.

Chapter 1. Parish church of San Francisco

1. Tello, *Crónica Miscelánea de la Sancta Provincia*; de Alba, *Chapala,* 31.
2. Ibid.
3. A photo and text "Se Recompensara a quien entregue una leona" by Don Armando Hermosillo, displayed in municipal archives in November 2017.
4. Ixca Farías, "Chapala", *El Informador,* 17 January 1937.
5. Lawrence, *The Plumed Serpent,* chapters XVI and XVIII.
6. De Alba, *Chapala,* 125.

Chapter 2. Stagecoaches and 1907 traffic congestion

1. Tweedie, *Mexico as I Saw It,* 249-250.
2. Terry, *Terry's Mexico Handbook,* 152.
3. *The Mexican Herald,* 13 May 1899, 5.
4. AHMC, "Box: Ind y Com de Chapala 1884-1998". Stagecoach service was suspended 11 July 1904; *Jalisco Times,* 16 September 1904.
5. *The Mexican Herald,* 4 Oct 1900; *El Tiempo,* 11 October 1900, 3.
6. *Jalisco Times,* 2 Jan 1904; 6 Feb 1904.
7. *El Imparcial: diario ilustrado de la mañana,* 19 April 1908; *The Mexican Herald,* 28 April 1910, 8.
8. De Alba, *Chapala,* 124.

Chapter 3. Gran Hotel Chapala (Posada Doña Trini)

1. *El Demócrata*, 27 April 1895, 4.
2. Ixca Farías. 1937. "Chapala", 6, 12.
3. *Jalisco Times*, 30 April 1904.
4. *El Paso Times*, 25 October 1905, 8.
5. *Jalisco Times*, 20 April 1906.
6* Adverts in *Jalisco Times* from at least as early as 11 Jan 1907.
7* *Jalisco Times*, 22 Feb 1907; 15 Mar 1907; 26 Apr 1907; 17 May 1907.
8* De Alba, *Chapala*, 123-4; *El Informador*, 8 October 1918, 2.
9* *El Informador*, 14 March 1919, 2.
10* Medina Loera, "Camino a Chapala;" Balch, "From Guadalajara, Take the Wichita Line..."
11. *El Correo de Jalisco*, 9 January 1907.
12. *El Informador,* 30 November 1919; 7 March 1920, 10.
13. *El Informador*, 30 March 1923; 8 April 1923, 5.
14. *El Informador*, 25 March 1925, 8.

Chapter 4. Villa Ana Victoria

1. *The Mexican Herald*, 12 December 1896, 5.
2. *The Mexican Herald*, 11 April 1897.
3. E.K.H., "Beautiful Chapala".
4. Ochoa Corona, "Chapala con problemas de estacionamiento..."

Chapter 5. The Widow's Bar

1. Chente García, "Chapala."
2. Death certificate.
3* The southern tower has an inscription that reads "comenzada y concluida en 1878." The clock above the main entrance was added in about 1897.
4* The eruption was from 20–24 January 1913.
5* A photo and text "Se Recompensara a quien entregue una leona" by Don Armando Hermosillo, displayed in municipal archives in November 2017.
6. Ficke, *Mrs. Morton of Mexico.*
7. Fisher, *The Gastronomical Me*, 556.
8. Parmenter, *Stages in a Journey*, 83.
9. Ciudad Real, *Tratado curioso y docto...".* See *Lake Chapala Through the Ages*, chapter 6.

Chapter 6. Casa Barragán (the Witter Bynner house)

1. Palomar, "Chapala: primera de las cuatro casas..."
2. Fuller. *Never a Dull Moment.*
3* Rispa and Toca, *Barragan: The Complete Works.*
4. Nehls, Edward (ed). 1958. *D. H. Lawrence: A Composite Biography. Volume Two, 1919-1925.* University of Wisconsin Press.

5. E.G., "Indian Earth."
6. Fuller. *Never a Dull Moment*.

Chapter 7. Plazas, old and new

1. *The Mexican Herald*, 12 December 1898.
2. AHMC unpublished timeline entry for 15 March 1910.
3. See *Western Mexico*, chapter 2, and *Lake Chapala Through the Ages*.
4. de Szyszlo, *Dix mille kilomètres...*, 235-236; translation by Marie-Josée Bayeur.
5. See the short illustrated booklet by Javier Raygoza and Gilberto Padilla García, published online by Página, Que sí se lee! at https://issuu.com/chapalavirtual/docs/libro_casa_verde [19 January 2020]

Chapter 8. Cerro San Miguel

1. Mota Padilla, *Historia del reino de Nueva Galicia*; Tello, *Crónica Miscelánea de la Sancta Provincia*.
2. *Book Buyer*, June 1900; *San Francisco Call*, Vol 87, No 108, 16 Sep. 1900.
3. Embree, *A Dream of a Throne*. For more about Embree's time in Chapala, see my *Lake Chapala through the ages*, chapter 43, and "American novelist Charles Fleming Embree."
4. *Jalisco Times*, 6 March 1908.
5. *El Informador*, 2 July 1931, 2.

Chapter 9. Old Municipal Building

1. Palfrey. "Old Chapala town hall."

Chapter 10. Municipal Building (Hotel Palmera, Hotel Nido)

1. *El Paso Times* reprinted in *The Oasis* (Arizola, Arizona), 9 June 1900, 10.
2. *El Correo de Jalisco*, 12 Apr 1907.
3. de Alba, *Chapala*, 116.
4. Dollero, *México al día*.
5. *El Informador*, 25 March 1925, 8.
6. Cristina, *El Chapala de Natalia*, 42-43.
7. One of the earliest ads for Hotel Nido is in *El Informador*, 8 May 1930, 6.
8. Félix, *Todas mis Guerras*. Quoted in Tipton, "María Felix: The Fantasy of the World," an article originally published on Judy King's website mexico-insghts. com. The star did visit the town in 1938, the year she and Álvarez divorced.
9. Casillas, *La Villa de Chapala*, 121. Casillas' earlier (almost identical) account of Mina's wedding, in *La Plaza* in 1987 does not name the villa.
10. Cristina, *El Chapala de Natalia*, 42-46.
11. *Modern Mexico* Vol 14, no 3 (August 1941), 25.

Chapter 11. Hotel Arzapalo

1. This misconception may stem from a misreading of this admittedly ambiguous sentence in Antonio de Alba, *Chapala*, p 116: "A los 7 años,

habiendo progresado la empresa, edifice el mismo Sr. Arzapalo, bajo la dirección del Ing. Guillermo de Alba otro hotel, el "Hotel Palmera". (After 7 years, the business having progressed, the same Mr Arzapalo built, under the direction of Engineer Guillermo de Alba another hotel the "Hotel Palmera.") Antonio de Alba never mentions Guillermo de Alba elsewhere in connection with either Ignacio Arzapalo or the Hotel Arzapalo. María Dolores Traslaviña García attempts to reconcile the discrepancy between the date the hotel was built and when de Alba was reportedly in Chicago by suggesting that the hotel opened prior to 1898 and that de Alba worked only on the second floor. No evidence has surfaced for either of these suggestions.

2. *El Tiempo*, 11 September 1896, 2.

3. F.R.G., "From Chapala."

4* My previous attempts to summarize Arzapalo's life were hopelessly inaccurate. While this account still leaves many unanswered questions, perhaps it will inspire others to fill in the gaps.

5* Arzapalo married his first wife, 16-year-old Emilia Salgado Maldonado, in Mazatlán in 1863; their twin daughters, Emilia and María Luisa, were born in Tepic four years later.

6* *El Siglo Diez y Nueve*, 8 April 1881; *Anales del Ministerio de Fomento de la República Mexicana*, Volume 4, 1881.

7* *La Voz de México*, 14 November 1888.

8* *La Voz de México*, 27 September 1888.

9. *The Mexican Herald* 20 March 1898, 5.

10. Goff, "Consumptives' Health Resort."

11. *El Tiempo*, 11 September 1896, 2.

12. *The Mexican Herald*, 27 March 1898. Guillermo de Alba is not mentioned in this report.

13. *The Mexican Herald*, 15 March 1898, 4.

14. *The Mexican Herald*, 13 May 1899, 5.

15. The earliest of these ads is in *The Mexican Herald*, 2 December 1899, 1.

16. *The Mexican Herald*, 11 January 1899, 5.

17. *La Patria*, 12 August 1904, 2.

18. *El Imparcial* (Mexico), 20 August 1910.

19. *La Patria potestad y la tutela testamentaria. Últimas constancias del juicio ordinario en que se han declarado nulas varias cláusulas del testamento del Sr. D. Ignacio Arzapalo, y en consecuencia, que la niña Aurora Arzapalo y Pérez Verdía se encuentra bajo La Patria potestad de su abuelo materno, el Sr. Lic. D. Luis Pérez Verdía. Guadalajara: Editorial Escuela Tipográfica Salesiana. 1912.*

20. *The Sun* (New York City), 20 June 1909, 13; *The Ocala Evening Star* (Florida), 23 June 1909.

21. Ibid.

22. *El Informador*, 22 September 1918, 4; 29 September 1918, 6.

23. *El Informador*, 14 March 1919, 2.

24. *El Informador*, 16 August 1926, 1.

Chapter 12. Beer Garden

1. *El Informador*, 13 April 1933, 4.
2. Cristina, *El Chapala de Natalia*, 34.
3. Laure, born in El Salto in 1937, began singing jazz, dance tunes and rock-and-roll at the Beer Garden in the mid-1950s. Known as "El Rey del Trópico", he had a long-term contract to sing there with his group Los Cometas. Among his best-loved songs was "Amor en Chapala". Laure had released 47 albums by the time of his death in 2000. A fine statue of the famous singer was added to the lakefront promenade in Chapala about a decade ago.
4. Former clients listed on the 2017 menu of the Beer Garden include President Gustavo Díaz Ordáz; state governors Guillermo Cosio Vidaurri, Francisco Medina Ascencio, Alberto Orozco Romero; and film stars Emilion "El Indio" Fernández, Eulalio González "El Piporro", María Félix "La Doña", Los Hermanos Soler, Antonio Aguilar, Roberto Cañedo and Arturo de Córdoba.
5. de Alba, *Chapala*, 109.
6. *El Informador*, 17 Oct 1918, 1.

Chapter 13. Casa Capetillo

1. Casa Capetillo, almost certainly one of the homes referred to by Eduardo A. Gibbon in 1893, is mentioned in newspapers from 1896.
2. *The Mexican Herald*, 12 December 1898.
3. Cristina, *El Chapala de Natalia*, 81.
4. *El Informador*, 25 May 1927, 5; 3 November 1927, 7; 15 December 1927, 7.
5. Online advert at https://cb.chapala.com/index.php/properties listing/ item/549-villa-antigua-1880 [19 January 2019]
6. *El Informador*, 16 June 1937, 3 (editorial).

Chapter 14. Casa Galván (Villa Aurora)

1. *Jalisco Times*, 18 June 1904.
2. *El Imparcial*, 19 April 1908; Ixca Farías, "Chapala."
3* *The Mexican Herald*, 21 May 1899, 7.
4* *The Mexican Herald*, 15 November 1903, 9; 18 July 1904; 18 September 1904; 18 November 1905.
5* *El Paso Herald*, 24 June 1907, 6; *The Mexican Herald*, 13 July 1907.
6* *The Mexican Herald*, 14 September 1908, 10.
7* Christian Schjetnan. 1932. Letter dated 29 April 1932 to *The New York Times*, published 6 May 1932. Note that the League of Nations was founded in 1920 and the United Nations established in 1945.
8. CMAC, historial catastral for Villa Aurora.

Chapter 15. Mi Pullman

1. AHMC, unpublished time line, entry for 29 May 1899.
2. CMAC, historial catastral.

3* The main sources are Casillas, *La Villa de Chapala*; Castillas, *¡Salvemos a Chapala!* and Alvarez del Castillo (coord), *Arquitecto Guillermo de Alba*.
4* *El Continental*, 18 August 1895, 3.
5* F.R.G., "From Chapala."
6* *La Patria*, 22 June 1906, 1.
7* *El Informador*, 19 November 1917, 4.
8* Casillas, *¡Salvemos a Chapala!*, 157.
9. Chenery, "Mi Pullman."

Chapter 16. Villa Ave María

1. This part was purchased from Gertrudis Mancilla, María de la Luz Mancilla de Fernández and María de la Luz Hernández (CMAC, historial catastral).

Chapter 17. Chalet Paulsen (Villa Paz)

1. *La Tierra*, 1 June 1901, 125-6.
2. *El Tiempo*, 23 September 1893.
3. Partida-Rocha, "Diario de un snob," *El Informador*, 12 December 2016.
4. *The San Francisco Call*, 16 December 1896, 5; *The Mexican Herald*, 12 December 1896, 5.
5* Taylor, "Old Orange County Courthouse."
6* *Los Angeles Herald*, 8 October 1900, 5.
7* *Jalisco Times* 13 June 1908; 17 October 1908.
8. *La Tierra*, 1 June 1901, 125-6; AHMC, unpublished time line, entry dated 25 April 1905.
9. AHMC, unpublished time line, entries for 1 April 1903 and 30 Sept 1903; *Jalisco Times*, 2 January 1904.
10. *The Mexican Herald,*, 29 October 1902, 5.
11. *Jalisco Times* 24 January 1908.
12. They married in Guadalajara on 21 April 1904.
13. Ownership details from CMAC, historial catastral for the property.

Chapter 18. Las Delicias therapeutic baths

1. Tello. *Crónica Miscelánea de la Sancta Provincia*. See ny *Lake Chapala Through the Ages*, chapter 2.
2. Baylor, "Lovely Lake Chapala."
3. *El Tiempo*, 21 April 1908.
4. US Consular Reports of Marriages, 1910–1949 (database on ancestry.com).
5. Fisher, *The Gastronomical Me*, 545.

Chapter 19. Villa Ferrara

1. Allera Mercadillo (coord), *Las villas de descanso*, 39.
2. Anita González Rubio y de la Torre had married José Cuervo; she managed Tequila Cuervo after her husband's death in 1921. When she died in 1934, the company passed to her niece, Lupe Gallardo González Rubio (1897–1964).

3. Center for Creative Photography, The University of Arizona, Tucson. Finding aid for the Esther Born collection, 1935–1937.

4* Palomar Verea, "Contra la amnesia tapatía"; Solano, "Retoman arquitectura religiosa"; and Allera Mercadillo (coord), *Las villas de descanso.*

5* Palomar Verea, "Pedro Castellanos, el urbanista."

6. Allera Mercadillo (coord), *Las villas de descanso,* 42.

7. de Alba, Chapala, 115-116; Casillas, *¡Salvemos a Chapala!* 83.

Chapter 20. Mineral water bottling plant

1. Unconfirmed Facebook comment by Angel Pérez Arce Sanabria, dated 3 January 2016.

2. Advert in *Crónica,* 1 December 1907, *Crónica* Año 1, #23, cited in Casillas, *La Villa de Chapala,* 136.

3. Cristina, *El Chapala de Natalia,* 15.

4. AHMC. 2016. "Las Limonadas de los Pérez Arce."

5. Salvador Pérez Arce Jr. was Presidente Municipal of Chapala in 1910.

6. Cristina, *El Chapala de Natalia,* 66.

7. Cristina, *El Chapala de Natalia,* 16.

8. Cristina, *El Chapala de Natalia,* 16.

Chapter 21. Villa Tlalocan

1. *The Two Republics,* 2 December 1885.

2* Dr. Ben Brown of the Museo de la Revolución, Cd. Juárez, personal communication.

3* *The Mexican Herald,,* 8 November 1908.

4* *Jalisco Times,* 2 January 1904.

5. *El Tiempo* (Mexico City), 11 September 1895.

6. *El Tiempo,* 5 May 1896.

7. *The Mexican Herald,* 12 December 1896, 5.

8. *El Nacional,* 24 April, 1897.

9. E.K.H., "Beautiful Chapala."

10. F.R.G. "Chapala Again."

11. *The Mexican Herald,* 4 December 1898.

12. *El Tiempo,* 24 February 1899.

13. *La Patria,* 1 March 1899, 3.

14. *The Mexican Herald,,* 12 March 1899, 2; *El Paso Herald,* 15 March 1899.

15. *La Patria,* 15 April 1899, 3.

16* *El Paso Times,* 07 May 1895, 7; *El Tiempo* (Mexico City) 11 September 1895.

17* *The Mexican Herald,* 12 December 1903, 5.

18* Johnson, "The Ruins of Mitla."

19* Young, *A History of the American British Cowdray Hospital,* 9-10.

20. Karl Ferdinand Eisenmann Schloss (known as Carlos Eisenmann in Mexico) was born in Berlin on 23 August 1853; he married Amelia Brígida Jordán

Aguilar (c. 1862–1933) in 1881. They had eight children, two of whom did not survive to adulthood.

21. Romero Gil, *El Boleo: Santa Rosalía*.
22. *Mexican Financier*, October 1889.
23. *The Mexican Herald*, 6 August 1899, 5.
24. *The Mexican Herald*,, 12 March 1899, 2.
25. *The Mexican Herald*,, 1 August 1899, 8.
26. de Alba, *Chapala*, 115; Martínez Réding, *Chapala*, 42; Boehm Schoendube, "El Lago de Chapala."
27. CMAC, historial catastral for Villa Tlalocan. This transfer, on 7 June 1917, is the earliest one recorded.
28. *El Paso Herald*, 8 June 1918, 20.
29. CMAC, historial catastral for Villa Tlalocan. The two transfers were on 2 January 1925 and 39 November 1925 respectively.
30. CMAC, historial catastral for Villa Tlalocan.

Chapter 22. Villa Adriana

1. Juan Palomar. 2018. "Para escándalo barraganesco."
2. Juan Palomar, personal communication, 2018.
3. J. Jesús González Gortázar. 1992. *Aquellos tiempos en Chapala*.

Chapter 23. Casa Albión (Villa Josefina)

1. *The Mexican Herald*, 12 December 1896, 5.
2. *The Mexican Herald*,, 12 March 1899.
3. F.R.G., "Chapala Again"; and *The Mexican Herald*, 19 August 1896.
4. Schafer (ed), *Memoirs of Jeremiah Curtin*, 527.
5. *The Mexican Herald*, 12 December 1896, 5.
6* The main source for biographical details of the Schnaider family is Cazares Puente, *Joseph Maximilian Schnaider: Industria, Cerveza y familia*.
7* *Jalisco Times*, 23 January 1904; 18 June 1904.
8. *The Mexican Herald*, 22 March 1897.
9. *The Mexican Herald*, 3 July 1898, 5.
10. *The Mexican Herald*, 12 December 1896, 5.
11. *The Mexican Herald*, 30 July 1903.
12. Farías, "Chapala."
13. Reply dated 20 May 1897 from Septimus Crowe to the Secretary of the Municipio of Chapala, in response to Notice #488. Original in AHMC.
14. *Jalisco Times*, 13 February 1904; *Jalisco Times*, 27 August 1904.
15. Cristina, *El Chapala de Natalia*, 66.
16. *El Pueblo*, 28 February 1916, 1; 1 March 1916, 1,8.
17. Hunziger is best known for directing the silent movie *The Tiger's Coat* (1920) which starred Tina Modotti, the beautiful Italian photographer-actress who had strong and intimate connections to Mexico and to Diego Rivera.
18. *El Informador*, 25 June 1922, 7.

19. See Burton, "Art Mystery."
20. Rogelio Ochoa Corona, personal communication.

Chapter 24. Villa Niza

1. (photo) F.R.G., "From Chapala."
2. The link to Somellera comes from García, "Chapala," 36. This particular Andrés Somellera (one of several in overlapping generations of this large family) is thought to be Andrés Somellera y Martínez Gallardo (1874–1944), the son of Agapito Somellera and María Martínez Gallardo.
3. This claim is made, for example, in Casillas, *La Villa de Chapala*, 82 and in Allera Mercadillo (coord), *Las villas de descanso*, 35.
4. *El Informador*, 24 November 1919, 5.
5. Schoendube, *Cartografía Histórica del Lago de Chapala*, archivo PDZF04.jpg.
6. The photo is used to illustrate Martín Casillas, "Volver a visitar Chapala."
7. García, "Chapala." The Oscar Newton in question is Oscar Newton Riebeling (1884-1964), son of Federico Augusto Newton Griswold (1826-1906) and María Dolores Epigmenia Riebeling Rivera (1847-1934).
8. AHMC, copy of land sale record dated 4 March 1941. My thanks to Rogelio Ochoa Corona for locating this document.

Chapter 25. Jardín del Mago

1. Palomar, "Para escándalo barraganesco."
2. Ibid.

Chapter 26. Villa Reynera

1. The iconic photo of Villa Reynera (photographer and date unknown), used for the cover of my *Lake Chapala Through the Ages*, shows an unidentified family group relaxing in the garden of this magnificent house.
2. The style is pre-1910. An early photo of the house includes a handwritten date of December 1911; the house was named on an official 1919 map.
3. *El Informador*, 12 December 1924, 4, 6.
4. Nauollin, a curious choice of title, presumably derived from Nahui Olin, the name adopted by Carmen Mondragón, the stunningly-beautiful, nymphomaniac lover of the famous painter Dr. Atl (Gerardo Murillo).
5. *Guadalajara Reporter,* 23 September 1977.
6. Unpublished letter, dated 14 July 1925, from Zara to Idella Purnell in personal archive of Purnell's daughter, Dr. Marijane Osborn.
7. *East-West*, Vol. 2 #4 (May-June 1927); Vol4 #3, (Nov-December 1929); de Brundige, *Quilocho*, 310.
8. Neill James. Unpublished manuscript entitled "Mexican Story", dated 26 October 1948, in NJA of LCS.
9. de Brundige, *Quilocho*.
10. Holger died in a nursing home in Guadalajara on 10 August 1944, well before his 50th birthday; his remains were interred in Ajijic cemetery.

11. Cristina, *El Chapala de Natalia*, 70.
12. Over the years (as recently as 2018) the street signs have used the inaccurate "Crow" as often as the correct "Crowe."

Chapter 27. La Capilla de Lourdes

1. Land records for Villa Francia, a 7232-square-meter estate close to the chapel at Calle Mónaco #5, show that Aurelio González Hermosillo bought land between 1903 and 1907 from Abraham Antolín, Juan Romulado Antolín, Francisco Fernández del Avalle (sic), J. Cruz Gómez, Polonio López, Bibiana Márquez, Dolores Nicasio, Sebastián Sainz, Florentina Siordia, Hipólita Siordia, Inocencia Siordia, and Leopoldo Walkupp.
2. de Alba, *Chapala*, 114.
3. Jack McDonald, writing in *Guadalajara Reporter,* 15 March 1975.
4. A plaque in the church to this effect is referred to in AHMC, unpublished time-line, entry for 1941.
5. Juan Palomar Verea, personal communication (email 26 August 2018), and Orozco, "Nuestra Señora de Lourdes."
6. Orozco, "Nuestra Señora de Lourdes."
7* Palomar Verea, "Juan Palomar y Arias."
8* Palomar Verea, "Pedro Castellanos."

Chapter 28. Hotel Villa Montecarlo

1. José Martín Rascón, born in about 1833, died 19 February 1893 in the Palace Hotel, San Francisco, en route back to Mexico from Japan.
2* Jane Rees, personal communication. Rees, Septimus Crowe's great-granddaughter, kindly shared a significant amount of valuable information about Crowe's life and family.
3* *El Minero Mexicano*, 16 June 1887, 3; 12 June 1890; *The Two Republics*, 25 December 1891.
4* *El Tiempo*, 23 June 1896; *The Mexican Herald*, 21 July 1896; *La Voz de México*, 19 August 1896.
5. *Times-Democrat* (New Orleans), 5 January 1896, 13.
6. Also present at that meeting, as the official representative for Jalisco, was Luis Pérez Verdía, who later built "Casa Braniff."
7. *The Mexican Herald*, 12 December 1896.
8. *The Mexican Herald*, 15 March 1898.
9. *The Mexican Herald*, 22 March 1897.
10. Gideon Townsend, born 1826, died 30 May 1899.
11. Mary Ashley Townsend, born in 1832, died 7 June 1901.
12. Baylor, "Lovely Lake Chapala."
13. *La Tierra*, 1 June 1901, 125-6.
14. *Jalisco Times*, 30 Apr 1904. The correct spelling of her birth name is Mary Ashley Van Voorhis (born 24 September 1832 in Lyons, New York).
15. AHMC, unpublished time line, entry for 5 June 1905.

16. Ochoa Corona, "Hoteleria y Villa Montecarlo."

17* Arq. Fernando Brizuela, personal communication, August 2018.

18* Cortés Lugo de Torres, *Recordando un Paraíso*.

19* *El Imparcial*, 23 September 1899, 1.

20* *La Iberia*, 2 June 1906, 2.

21* *La Voz de México*, 26 February 1907, 1.

22. *El Informador*, 15 December 1918, 6; 16 December 1918, 1.

23. *El Informador*, 18 February 1919, 5.

24. González Casillas, "El "habitat" de los tapatíos de ayer."

25. *El Informador*, 5 June 1925.

26. The property was legally transferred to his widow, María Josefina Brizuela Ornelas (1866 1942), on 20 June 1928. CMAC, historial catastral.

27. *El Informador*, 24 April 1932.

28. *El Informador*, 29 April 1934.

29. *El Informador*, 31 May 1935; *El Informador*, 19 October 1935, 1.

30. Burton, "Art Mystery." Translation of letter kindly supplied by Mona Lang.

31. Sybille Bedford. 1953. *The Sudden View: A Mexican journey*. (London: Victor Gollancz Ltd., & New York: Harper & Brothers); revised edition published as *A Visit to Don Otavio: A Traveller's Tale from Mexico*, (London: Collins, 1960).

32. Fernando Partida Rocha, personal communication.

33. *El Informador*, 18 November 1944; 22 August 1948.

34. *El Informador*, 3 February 1948.

35. Bashford, *Tourist Guide to Mexico*; List of foreign residents in Chapala, June 1955, a document in LCS archives, kindly supplied by LCS Archivist.

36. *Guadalajara Reporter*, 22 January 1977, 17.

37. *Guadalajara Reporter*, 22 October 1964; 29 October 1964. *El Informador*, 31 October 1964.

38. CMAC, historial catastral for Villa Montecarlo.

Chapter 29. Villa Bela (Villa Bell)

1. No evidence has yet surfaced that the villa was ever connected to Crowe's fellow Englishman Richard Bell (1858–1911), a circus clown who rose to prominence in Mexico at the end of the nineteenth century. Bell moved to the US shortly before his death. From about 1912 to 1920, his widow joined with their thirteen children—and their respective spouses and offspring, some of whom lived in Guadalajara—to tour Latin America and elsewhere as The Bell Vaudeville.

2. Boehm Schoendube (coord.), *Cartografía Histórica del Lago de Chapala*, Archivo PDZF04.jpg.

3. de Alba, *Chapala*, 119-120.

4. CMAC, historial catastral. I am especially grateful to Rogelio Ochoa Corona, the former Municipal Archivist in Chapala, and the staff of the Land Registry for locating this information.

5. Ibid.

6. *The Mexican Herald*, 8 May 1902.

Chapter 30. La Casita Blanca

1. *Middletown Times*, Middletown, New York, 8 Feb 1939, 7.

2. *Philadelphia Inquirer*, 14 June 1952, 5; *The Morning News*, Wilmington, Delaware, 9 Dec 1949, 36.

3. McCombe, "Yanks Who Don't Go Home."

4. Scott, "Over One Thousand Children."

Chapter 31. Villa Virginia

1. *The Mexican Herald*, 11 April 1897.

2. Hale, *Roots in Virginia*.

3. Harriet Doerr. 1984. *Stones for Ibarra*. New York: The Viking Press.

4. Martínez Delgado, *Cambio y Proyecto Urbano*, 141.

5. CMAC, historial catastral. The land had previously been owned by Doris Vest de Jaacks, the mother of Juan Jaacks, who had inherited her son's extensive property portfolio three years after he was murdered in Ajijic in 1896.

6. *The Mexican Herald*, 8 February 1911, 9.

7. Grace was the only surviving child of his first marriage, though he subsequently had nine other children with his second wife.

8. *The San Antonio Daily Express*, 28 May 1909, 2. Other accounts include *La Opinion*, 25 May 1909.

9. Katie Goodridge Ingram, personal communication via email, 31 May 2015.

10. Virginía Anne Hunton, born in 1942, died on 10 April 1944.

11. McDonald, "Inn's Charming Hostess."

12. Arthur Davison Ficke. 1939. *Mrs Morton of Mexico*. New York: Reynal & Hitchcock.

13. *Sybille Bedford. A Sudden View* (London: Victor Gollancz, 1953); reissued as *A Visit to Don Otavio* (William Collins, 1960).

14. McDonald, "Inn's Charming Hostess."

15. Ibid.

16. Katie Goodridge Ingram, personal communication via email, 31 May 2015.

17. *El Informador*, 30 August 1959, 1-2. Other entrants included the novelist Ramón Rubín and Carlos Winsnes, the Norwegian engineer who supervised construction of the La Capilla-Chapala railroad.

18. *El Informador*, 7 October 1959, 3.

19. *El Informador*, 25 November 1971.

20. *Guadalajara Reporter*, 27 June 1970.

21. CMAC, historial catastral.

Chapter 32. Villa Macedonia and the Schmoll residence

1. *El Informador*, 24 November 1919, 5.

2. García, "Chapala," 37.

3. *El Informador*, 28 July 1918, 6; 18 March 1944, 10.
4. *El Informador*, 24 November 1919, 5. For details of Schmoll's life and work, see my "Artist and cactus collector Ferdinand Schmoll (1879 1950)," www.lakechapalaartists.com/?p=2231.
5. *El Informador*, 11 December 1921, 5.

Chapter 33. Villa Tatra

1. Melby, "Among Lakeside's Most Illustrious."
2. Unpublished note dated 19 November 1966 in Lake Chapala Society's Neill James Archive.

Chapter 34. El Manglar

1. de Alba, *Chapala*, 117.
2. Bynner, *Journey with Genius*, 129-30.
3. McDonald, "Inn's Charming Hostess."
4. Mea culpa: I've repeated this claim several times in the past, too!
5. *The Mexican Herald*, 12 December 1896, 5; *The San Francisco Call*, 16 December 1896, 5.
6. Carmen Romero Rubio had been Díaz's English teacher prior to marrying the 51-year-old president in 1881, when she was barely 17 years old.
7. *Jalisco Times*, 23 January 1904.
8. *Jalisco Times*, 16 January 1904.
9. *Jalisco Times*, 23 January 1904.
10. *Evening Star* (Washington, D.C.), 25 April 1905, 9.
11. *El Popular*, 13 April 1906, 1; 16 April 1906, 2; *The Mexican Herald*, 26 March 1907, 2; *El Contemporáneo*, 27 March 1907, 2.
12. *El Popular*, 13 April 1906, 1; *The Mexican Herald*, 26 March 1907, 2.
13. *Jalisco Times*, 17 April 1908.
14. *El Imparcial*, 19 April 1908.
15. *El Tiempo*, 21 April 1908.
16. *El Paso Herald*, 4 September 1908.
17. *El Democrata fronterizo* (Laredo, Texas), 10 April 1909, 2.
18. de Szyszlo, *Dix mille kilomètres a travers le Mexique*, 242-244. Translation by Marie Josée Bayeur. See also chapter 55 of my *Lake Chapala Through the Ages*.
19. El Mundo Ilustrado, 3 April 1910; Casillas, *¡Salvemos a Chapala!* 84.
20. Comments on Facebook by Fernando Brizuela and Juan Carlos Ramirez Aguilar.
21. Everett Gee Jackson. 1985. *Burros and Paintbrushes, A Mexican Adventure*. Texas A&M University Press, 85.
22. Idem., 92.
23. Idem., 107.
24. Comments published on Facebook by Antonio Hermosillo V. and Fernando Brizuela.
25. Vuilleumier, "Lake Chapala, Hacienda El Manglar."

Chapter 35. Waterfront and original yacht club

1. This is probably the Manuel Henríquez who was a partner of Guillermo de Alba.
2. AHMC, unpublished time line entry for 27 November 1897.
3. AHMC, unpublished time line entries for 20 January 1898; 25 April 1898; 15 September 1898.
4. AHMC, unpublished time line entries for 3 April 1908, 13 June 1908 and 14 October 1908.
5. *Jalisco Times*, 18 June 1904; 27 August 1904.
6. *Jalisco Times*, 6 August 1904.
7. *St. Louis Post Dispatch* (Missouri) 19 March 1905, 26; *El Paso Herald*, 9 April 1910, 23.
8. The *Condor* is described and illustrated in Harry H. Dunn. 1911. "Sailing on tropical seas. Part XCC. On the Lakes of Old Mexico." *The Rudder* (New York), vol 25.
9. Uncatalogued document dated 18 November 1916 in AHMC.
10. Burton, "The sacred geography."
11. *The Mexican Herald*, 12 December 1896, 5.
12. *La Tierra*, 1 June 1901, 125-6.
13. *Jalisco Times*, 13 February 1904. *The Spokane Press*, (Spokane, Washington), 19 March 1904, 3.
14. *Jalisco Times*, 26 March 1904; 7 May 1904.
15. *Jalisco Times*, 6 September 1907; 8 September 1907, 5. *Unión Ibero Americana*, December 1907, 48.
16. *Jalisco Times*, 8 September 1907; *Greensboro Daily News*, 27 October 1907,
17. *Guadalajara Reporter*, 28 January 2016.
18. See several chapters in my *Lake Chapala Through the Ages* and chapter 2 of *Western Mexico, A Traveler's Treasury*.
19. *Jalisco Times*, 18 June 1904.
20. Charles Fleming Embree. 1900. *A Dream of a Throne, the Story of a Mexican Revolt*. Boston: Little, Brown and Company. For more about Embree's time in Chapala, see chapter 43 of my *Lake Chapala Through the Ages*, and "American novelist Charles Fleming Embree set his first novel at Lake Chapala" (MexConnect, 2009). www.mexconnect.com/articles/3464-american-novelist-charles-fleming-embree-set-his-first-novel-at-lake-chapala
21. Lawrence, *The Plumed Serpent*, chapter 6.
22. Palomar Verea, "Esplendores de Chapala".
23. AHMC, unpublished time line, entry for April 1950.

Chapter 36. Casa Braniff

1. Source quoted in Gabriel Pareyón. 2007. *Diccionario Enciclopédico de Música en México*. Zapopan, Jalisco: Universidad Panamericana, 2 volumes, as Alfredo Carrasco. 1939. *Mis recuerdos (colección de crónicas y apuntes)*.

Reprinted UNAM, 1997, 247-250. Original source is Ixca Farías. *Casos y cosas de mis tiempos*. Colegio Internacional. Guadalajara, 1963, 58-64.

2. XI Reunión del Congreso Internacional de Americanistas. 1895, XI Reunión en México, 15-20 October 1895.

3. Murià, "Luis Pérez Verdía."

4. *Jalisco Times*, 5 March 1904.

5. *Jalisco Times*, 12 March 1904.

6. *Jalisco Times*, 18 June 1904.

7. *Jalisco Times*, 3 September 1904.

8. AHMC, unpublished time line, entry for 5 June 1905.

9. Murià, "Luis Pérez Verdía."

10. Bynner, *Journey with Genius*, 93.

11. *Jalisco Times* 8 September 1907, 5.

12. Despite the coincidence of name and a shared interest in flying, Alberto Braniff and his brothers, Thomás and Arturo, were completely unrelated to the Thomas Elmer Braniff who co-founded Braniff Airlines in 1928 and which, at its peak, was the sixth-largest airline in the world.

13. Anon. "Alberto Braniff Ricard (1885–1966)". Website post at http://www.elbiplano.com/Braniff.html [20 July 2018]. Braniff's biplane crash occurred on 30 January 1910.

14. Farías, "Chapala."

15. CMAC, historial catastral for the property.

16. Palfrey, "Historic Buildings Reflect Chapala's Golden Era."

Chapter 37. Villa Robles León

1. Postcard dating from about 1925-1930 signed "Fot. S." (believed to be José Edmundo Sánchez).

2. Allera Mercadillo (coord), *Las villas de descanso*, 29.

3. Architect Juan Palomar, personal communication.

4. Allera Mercadillo (coord), *Las villas de descanso*, 61-66.

5. Letyvego Verplancken, comment on Facebook page "Imágenes históricas de Guadalajara," 4 April 2020.

Chapter 38. Villa Carmen

1. *The Mexican Herald*, 4 December 1898.

2. CMAC, historial catastral.

3. Antonio Barba was Presidente Municipal of Chapala in 1899, 1901 and 1904.

4. *El Informador*, 5 March 1972, 11-C ("Hace cincuenta años").

5. CMAC, historial catastral.

Chapter 39. Casa de las Cuentas (the D. H. Lawrence house)

1. Lawrence, *The Plumed Serpent*, chapter 9, entitled "Casa de las Cuentas." The tree is a soapberry (Sapindus saponaria); the seeds, which are toxic, are used for crafts, beadwork and rosaries.

2. Ibid.

3. Goldsmith, "A Week-end house in Mexico."

4. Ibid.

5. Nehls, *D. H. Lawrence*, note 118, 499.

6. Burton, "Roy MacNicol's adventurous life."

7. Mary MacNicol. 1967. *Flower Cookery: The Art of Cooking with Flowers*. New York: Fleet Press Corp.

8. *Guadalajara Reporter*, 6 July 1968; 26 October 1968.

9. Al Purdy. 1980. *The D.H. Lawrence House at Chapala*. The Paget Press.

10. Busam, John. 1994. "Inn of the Plumed Serpent." *Travelmex* (Guadalajara), No 114, 1-3.

Chapter 40. Villa Ochoa

1. Juan Palomar Verea, personal communication. Palomar Verea, "Esplendores de Chapala."

2. Juan Palomar Verea, personal communication.

3. Allera Mercadillo (coord), *Las villas de descanso*, 53.

4. *El Informador*, 8 June 1980, 35.

5. Allera Mercadillo (coord), *Las villas de descanso*, 31-32.

6. *The Mexican Herald*, 15 March 1898, 4.

7. Verónica Venegaz Muñoz. 2009. La Casa Ochoa. *El Informador*, 16 August 2009, 4-F.

8. Ibid.

Chapter 41. Chapala Yacht Club

1. *Jalisco Times*, 17 Apr 1908; *El Imparcial*, 19 April 1908.

2. *El Informador*, 26 March 1932, 1,2.

3. *New York Times*, 10 Nov 1947; *El Informador*, 6 November 1947, 13, 20.

4. *El Informador*, 11 October 1958.

5. *Guadalajara Reporter*, 1 February 1969.

6. *El Informador*, 3 March 1961, 13, 14.

7. *El Informador*, 18 March 1962, 13.

8. *El Informador*, 19 March 1963, 13.

Chapter 42. Chapala Railroad Station

1. *Daily Alta California*, 18 December 1866, 1; and documents pertaining to the "Compañía Anónima de Navegación del Lago de Chapala y Río Grande, 1866 1867" in Online Archive of California.

2. Eduardo W. Jackson was the CEO of Compañia Limitada del Ferrocarril Central Mexicano when the Irapuato-Guadalajara was being built; the company's attorney in Guadalajara was Luis Pérez Verdía.

3. Thomas L. Rogers, *Mexico? Sí, señor*, 157-159.

4. *El Correo Español*, 24 March 1900; de Alba, *Chapala*, 105, 172-3.

5. *El Mundo Ilustrado*, 27 March 1910.

6. An image of the drawing is included in Helbig, "El lago de Chapala en México."

7. *El Informador*, 11 August 1920.

8. Kenneth Bjork, "Saga in Steel and Concrete: Norwegian Engineers in America" (published by the Norwegian American Historical Association, NAHA), 1947. NAHA : http://www.naha.stolaf.edu

9. *The Mexican Herald*, 12 April 1913.

10. Brøgger, *Gullfeber*, 63. Note that segregation of rail cars was in effect in many US states, including Texas, at that time.

11. Idem., 63-64.

12. Idem., 64.

13. The company's constitution was approved on 20 February 1917. Details come from Valerio Ulloa, "Empresarios en Jalisco," 37 and footnote 21. Valerio cites Archivo de Instrumentos Públicos de Jalisco, Alfonso Mancilla. T.25, 20/02/1917.

14. *El Informador*, 19 September 1919.

15. Not "Wisnes", as sometimes appears in Spanish-language sources.

16. The original blueprints for this route were rediscovered in 2012 when students from Instituto Tecnológico y de Estudios Superiores de Occidente (ITESO) undertook a feasibility study for turning the route of the former rail line into a Via Verde ("Green Route") for hikers and cyclists.

17. *El Informador*, 9 August 1918.

18. *El Informador*, 15 September 1918, 2.

19. Galindo Gaitán, *Estampas de Chapala*, vol 1, 23.

20. *El Informador*, 24 June 1919.

21. Some trains had already used the new line. According to *El Informador*, 20 March 1920, 7, the first pullman car, a private car bringing Lic. Jose R Aspe, his family and friends from Mexico City, arrived in Chapala in mid-March.

22* *El Informador*, 29 December 1917, 2.

23* *Diario Oficial de la Federación*. 17 February 1922, 728-729. Secretaría de Comunicaciones y Obras Públicas. "Contrato celebrado con el señor Agustín Farías, para el arrendamiento de un terreno de zona federal y la explotación de unas casetas de madera para baño, en la Villa de Chapala, Estado de Jalisco."

24* *El Informador*, 6 May 1940, 4.

25* *Diario Oficial de la Federación*. 27 December 1944, 3-5. Secretaría de Marina. "Contrato concesión otorgado al señor ingeniero Birger Winsnes, para la explotación industrial del "Lirio", en las aguas de los ríos Sanitago y sus afluentes, en el Estado de Jalisco."

26. A full list can be found in Casillas, *La Villa de Chapala*, 64-66, and Casillas, *¡Salvemos a Chapala!* 239-242.

27. For an informative and entertaining account of this important day in Chapala's history, see Casillas, *La Villa de Chapala*, 62-78.

28. *El Informador*, advert, 10 November 1920.

29. *El Informador*, advert, 24 December 1920.

30. AHMC, unpublished time line, entry for 22 November 1922.

31. Boehm Schoendube (coord), *Cartografía Histórica del Lago de Chapala,* Archivo PDZF11.jpg.

32. Strictly speaking, the Norwegian capital was Christiania (1624–1877), then Kristiania (1877–1924), though the use of the old spelling continued informally for many years, before becoming Oslo from 1 January 1925.

33. Bynner, *Journey with Genius*, 90.

34. Cota 99.33 - the lake's cota (level) is measured in meters. Cota 100.00 was originally an arbitrarily chosen height on a long-since demolished bridge.

35. *El Informador*, 3 October 1926, 1. Schjetnan is not mentioned again in *El Informador* until 1932.

36. de Alba, *Chapala*, 122.

37. *El Informador*, 19 June 1940.

38. *El Informador*, 6 November 1947.

39. *Guadalajara Reporter*, 25 June 1964.

40. Palfrey, "First lady opens renovated train station."

Key dates, 1885–1970

1885? Septimus Crowe arrived in Mexico

1888 Branch of Mexican Central Railroad reached Ocotlán and Guadalajara

1890? Septimus Crowe built Villa Montecarlo

1893 Eduardo Gibbon described Chapala in print

1896 Septimus Crowe built Casa Albión

1896 Villa Tlalocan completed and occupied by Lionel Carden

1896 President Porfirio Díaz visited Chapala; almost lost his life in a storm

1898 Formal opening of Hotel Arzapalo

1898 Villa Ochoa completed

1900? Villa Paz completed

1901 Villa Bell built by Septimus Crowe

1903 Posada Doña Trini renamed the Hotel Victor Huber

1904 and 1905 President Díaz vacationed in Chapala

1905 Villa Pérez Verdía completed, sold to Braniff family in 1907

1905 Villa Virginia built by Hunton family

1906 Guillermo de Alba moved into Mi Pullman

1907 Hotel Palmera opened

1908 and 1909 President Díaz revisited Chapala

1910–1920 Mexican Revolution disrupted tourism

1910 Opening of (Old) Municipal building

1911 First Chapala Yacht Club inaugurated; it burned down in 1916

1917 Construction began of La Capilla-Chapala railroad

1919 Completion of Villa Niza

1920 La Capilla–Chapala Railroad and Chapala Railroad Station opened

1920 Start of a lakefront bar (later The Widow's Bar)

1923 D. H. Lawrence and Witter Bynner visited Chapala

1926 Serious floods in Chapala closed the Chapala Railroad Station

1926–1929 Cristeros Religious Rebellion disrupted tourism

1930 Formal opening of Hotel Nido

1931 Luis Barragán and Juan Palomar y Arias remodeled Barragán family home

1935 Building of Villa Ferrara

1941 Consecration of La Capilla de Lourdes

1942 Luis Barragán designed Jardin del Mago

1949–1951 Chapala town center was extensively remodeled

1954 Antonio de Alba published *Chapala*, his history of the town

1954–1955 Severe drought, the worst of the twentieth century

1955 Founding of the American Society (now the Lake Chapala Society)

1957 *Life* magazine article about Chapala and Ajijic

1967–1968 Lake level rose so high it caused major flooding

1970 Chapala (population 10,520) received city status

Sources of illustrations

Archives and periodicals

Archives consulted for this book included:

Acervo Histórico del Biblioteca Pública del Estado de Jalisco "Juan José Arreola."
Archivo Histórico del Agua.
Archivo Histórico Municipal de Chapala (municipal archive) (AHMC). An
  unpublished time line of events in Chapala, compiled by AHMC in about
  2005, and land records obtained by AHMC from the Catastro Municipal del
  Ayuntamiento de Chapala (CMAC) were especially valuable.
Colección José Y. Limantour, Centro de Estudios de Historia de México
  CARSO.
Hemeroteca Nacional Digital de México.
Lake Chapala Society Archive (LCS) and its Neill James Archive (NJA).

Periodicals:

The most useful Spanish-language periodical and newspaper sources, by title,
published in Mexico City unless otherwise indicated were:
El Continental (Guadalajara).
El informador (Guadalajara), 1917–present.
El Imparcial, 1899-1908.
El Mundo Ilustrado.
La Patria, 1899-1904.
La Voz de México, 1888-1907.
and the most useful English-language periodical and newspaper sources were:
The Mexican Herald (Mexico City), 1896–1908.
Jalisco Times (Guadalajara), 1904–1908.
New York Times.
The Guadalajara Reporter, 1963–present (TGR). For simplicity, this title is
  used throughout for the periodical previously known as *The Colony Reporter*
  (1963–1987) and *The Colony Guadalajara Reporter* (1987–2006).

Bibliography

Books, articles, blog posts

Allera Mercadillo, Juan G. Heriberto. 2015. *Las villas de descanso de Chapala*. Guadalajara: Tecnológico de Monterrey / Municipio de Chapala.

Alvarez del Castillo, Jaime (coordinator). 2002. *Arquitecto Guillermo de Alba*. Editorial Agata / Fotoglobo.

Anon. Undated. "Alberto Braniff Ricard (1885-1966)." Blog post at elbiplano. com/Braniff.html [20 July 2018].

Antonio de Alba. 1954. *Chapala*. Banco Industrial de Jalisco.

Balch, Trudy. 1991. "From Guadalajara, Take the Wichita Line..." *Guadalajara Reporter*, 23 November 1991, 3-4.

Bashford, G. M.. 1954. *Tourist Guide to Mexico*. McGraw-Hill.

Baylor, George Wythe. 1902. "Lovely Lake Chapala." *El Paso Herald*, 1 November 1902, 10. Reprinted as chapter 3 of George Wythe Baylor and Jerry D. Thompson. 1996. *Into the Far, Wild Country: True Tales of the Old Southwest*. Texas Western Press.

Bedford, Sybille. 1953. *The Sudden View: A Mexican journey*. (London: Victor Gollancz Ltd., & New York: Harper & Brothers); revised edition retitled *A Visit to Don Otavio: A Traveller's Tale from Mexico*. (London: Collins, 1960).

Bjork, Kenneth. 1947. "Saga in Steel and Concrete: Norwegian Engineers in America" (published by the Norwegian-American Historical Association, NAHA) at naha.stolaf.edu.

Boehm Schoendube, Brigitte (coord.) 2002. *Cartografía Histórica del Lago de Chapala* (CD), El Colegio de Michoacán.

———. 2001. "El Lago de Chapala: Su Ribera Norte. Un ensayo de lectura del paisaje cultural." *Relaciones* (Colegio de Michoacán), Vol 22 85, 2001, 58-83.

Brøgger, Kr. Fr. 1932. *Gullfeber - en advokats optegnelser fra siste jobbetid*. (Gold Fever - A Lawyer's Records from the last job.). Forlagt av H. Aschehoug & Co (W. Nygaard), 63-64. [translation by author]

Burton, Tony. 2009. *Lake Chapala through the ages; an anthology of travellers' tales*. Canada: Sombrero Books.

———. 2009. "American novelist Charles Fleming Embree set his first novel at Lake Chapala." mexconnect.com/articles/3464

———. 2013. "The sacred geography of the Mexico's Huichol Indians." Blog post dated 24 June 2013 at geo-mexico.com/?p=8547

———. 2013. *Western Mexico: A Traveler's Treasury* (4th edition). Canada: Sombrero Books.

———. 2015. "Roy MacNicol's adventurous life and artistic career." Blog post at lakechapalaartists.com/?p=3174

———. 2017. "Art Mystery: Whose portraits were painted by Swedish artist Nils Dardel when he visited Chapala in about 1941?" Blog post dated 7 December 2017 at lakechapalaartists.com/?p=6641 [21 August 2018].

Busam, John. 1994. "Inn of the Plumed Serpent." *Travelmex* (Guadalajara), No 114, 1-3.

Bynner, Witter. 1951. *Journey with Genius: Recollection and Reflections Concerning The D.H. Lawrences*. New York: The John Day Company.

Carrasco, Alfredo. 1939. *Mis recuerdos (colección de crónicas y apuntes)*. Reprinted UNAM, 1997, 247-250.

Casillas de Alba, Martín. 1987. "La Boda de Mina de Alba según ella la contaba." *La Plaza* (Guadalajara), Año 1, #7 (March 1987), 14-17.

———. 1994. *La Villa de Chapala: los promotores, sus inversiones y un inspirado escritor (1895-1933)*. Banco Promex, 136.

———. 2004. *¡Salvemos a Chapala!* Mexico: Editorial Diana.

———. 2014. "Volver a visitar Chapala", *El Informador,* 22 May 2014.

Cazares Puente, Eduardo. 2017. *Joseph Maximilian Schnaider: Industria, Cerveza y familia*. Monterrey: Kolektiva Editorial.

Chenery, Ros. 2009. "Mi Pullman: remodeling a Mexican Art Nouveau townhouse." Article at mexconnect.com/articles/3474 [20 January 2020]

Ciudad Real, Antonio de. c.1590. *Tratado curioso y docto de las grandezas de la Nueva Espana: Relacion breve y verdadera de algunas cosas de las muchas que sucedieron al padre fray Alonso Ponce en las provincias de la Nueva Espana...* 3rd edition, 1993. Mexico: UNAM Instituto de Investigaciones Historicas.

Cortés Lugo de Torres, Josefina. 2010. *Recordando un Paraíso*.

Cristina, Zaida (Zaida Cristina Reynoso Camacho). 2010. *El Chapala de Natalia*. Chapala: Ediciones Clavileño, 15.

de Brundige, Frances (pseudonym of Eleanore Saenger / Khyva St. Albans). 1973. *Quilocho and the Dancing Stars*. Philadelphia: Dorrance & Co.

de Szyszlo, Vitold. 1913. *Dix mille kilomètres a travers le Mexique, 1909-1910*. Paris: Plon-Nourrit et Cie., 242-244. Translation by Marie-Josée Bayeur. [See also LCTTA chapter 55]

Doerr, Harriet. 1984. *Stones for Ibarra*. New York: The Viking Press.

Dollero, Adolfo. 1911. *México al día (Impresiones y notas de viaje)*. Paris: Libreria de la Vda de C. Bouret.

Dunn, Harry H.. 1911. "Sailing on tropical seas. Part X_C. On the Lakes of Old Mexico." *The Rudder* (New York), vol 25.

E.G. 1929. "Indian Earth" (review). *Pacific Affairs* (University of British Columbia), Vol 2 #2 (Dec 1929), 804.

E.K.H. "Beautiful Chapala - Some Ripples from that lake", *The Mexican Herald*, 22 March 1897.

Embree, Charles Fleming. 1900. *A Dream of a Throne, the Story of a Mexican Revolt*. Boston: Little, Brown and Company.

F.R.G. 1898. "From Chapala: A Budding Watering-Place of Pleasant Promise." *The Mexican Herald*, 15 March 1898.

———. 1898. "Chapala Again." *The Mexican Herald*, 21 Mar 1898; 19 Aug 1896.

Farías, Ixca. 1937. "Chapala", *El Informador,* 17 January 1937, 6, 12; reprinted 22 December 1963, 2, 12.

———. 1963. *Casos y cosas de mis tiempos*. Ediciones del Colegio Internacional. Guadalajara.

Félix, María. 1994. *Todas mis Guerras*. Editorial Clío.

Ficke, Arthur Davison. 1939. *Mrs Morton of Mexico*. New York: Reynal & Hitchcock.

Fisher, Mary Frances Kennedy. 1979. *The Gastronomical Me*. Duell, Sloan and Pearce, New York), reprinted in *The Art of Eating*. Macmillan.

Fuller, Mark S.. 2015. *Never a Dull Moment: The Life of John Liggett Meigs*. Sunstone Press.

Galindo Gaitán, Manuel. 2003. *Estampas de Chapala*, vol 1. Guadalajara: Ediciones Pacífico, S.A.

García, Chente. 2002. "Chapala." Chapter 6 (33-38) in Jaime Alvarez del Castillo (coordinator). 2002. *Arquitecto Guillermo de Alba*. Guadalajara: Editorial Agata/Fotoglobo.

Gibbon, Eduardo A. 1893. *Guadalajara, (La Florencia Mexicana). El salto de Juanacatlán y El Mar Chapálico*. 1992 reprint Guadalajara: Presidencia Municipal de Guadalajara.

Goff, Ella D.. 1895. "Consumptives' Health Resort for the Entire Year (All Seasons)" in *Transactions of the Homeopathic Medical Society, State of Pennsylvania*.

Goldsmith, Margaret O. (1941) "Week-end house in Mexico." *House and Garden* vol 79 (May 1941) p. sup 44-45.

González Casillas, Magdalena. 1987. "El "habitat" de los tapatíos de ayer," *El Informador*, 8 Feb 1987, 87-88.

González Gortázar, J. Jesús. 1992. *Aquellos tiempos en Chapala*. Guadalajara: Editorial Agata.

Hale, Nathaniel Claiborne. 1948. *Roots in Virginia : an account of Captain Thomas Hale, Virginia frontiersman....* George H. Buchanan Company, 54/55. https://catalog.hathitrust.org/Record/005695119 [2 February 2019]

Helbig, Karl. 2003. "El lago de Chapala en México y su desecamiento." *Boletín del Archivo Histórico del Agua*, N_. 24, 2003, pags. 27-47.

Jackson, Everett Gee. 1985. *Burros and Paintbrushes, A Mexican Adventure*. Texas A&M University Press.

Johnson, C. G.. 1904. "The ruins of Mitla, Mexico." *Journal of the Royal Institute of British Architects*, (Vol 11, Third Series, 24 September 1904) 513-525.

Lawrence, D. H. 1926. *The Plumed Serpent*. London: Martin Secker Ltd.

MacNicol, Mary. 1967. *Flower Cookery: The Art of Cooking with Flowers*. New York: Fleet Press Corp.

Martínez Delgado, Gerardo. 2017. *Cambio y Proyecto Urbano. Aguascalientes 1880-1914*. Aguascalientes: Universidad Autónoma de Aguascalientes, 141.

Martínez Réding, Fernando. 1973. *Chapala*. Guadalajara: Jalisco Turista S.A.

McCombe, Leonard. 1957. "Yanks Who Don't Go Home. Expatriates Settle Down to Live and Loaf in Mexico." *Life Magazine*, 23 December 1957.

McDonald, Jack. 1968. "Inn's Charming Hostess is Chapala "Native"." *Guadalajara Reporter*, 29 June 1968, 12.

Medina Loera, Javier. 1991. "Camino a Chapala: del trazo de carretas a la autopista." *El Informador*, 17 March 1991, 37.

Melby, Arthur. 2005. "Among Lakeside's Most Illustrious..." *Ojo del Lago*, January 2005, Volume 21, Number 5.

Mota Padilla, Matias de la. 1742. *Historia del reino de Nueva Galicia en la América Septentrional*. Modern edition: 1973 Guadalajara, Mexico: Universidad de Guadalajara Instituto Jalisciense de Antropología e Historia.

Murià, José María. 1982. "Luis Pérez Verdía", *Historia de Jalisco*, vol 4, 24. Gobierno del Estado de Jalisco.

Nehls, Edward (ed). 1958. *D. H. Lawrence: A Composite Biography. Volume Two, 1919-1925*. University of Wisconsin Press.

Ochoa Corona, Rogelio. 2016 (a), "Chapala con problemas de estacionamiento en la época del Porfiriato." *Laguna*, 27 May 2016. http://semanariolaguna. com/17441/ [21 July 2018]

———. 2016 (b). "Las Limonadas de los Pérez Arce." *Laguna*, 17 June 2016. http://semanariolaguna.com/17917/

———. 2016 (c). "Hoteleria y Villa Montecarlo." *Laguna*, 17 Sep 2016. semanariolaguna.com/20086/ [20 Aug 2018]

Orozco, Luis Enrique. 1958. "Nuestra Señora de Lourdes de Chapala. Reseña histórica ordenada por el Sr. Cura D. Raúl Navarro, como un homenaje de la Parroquia de Chapala a la Madre de Dios, en el primer centenario de sus apariciones en la gruta de Lourdes, Francia." Guadalajara.

Palfrey, Dale Hoyt. 2004. "Historic Buildings Reflect Chapala's Golden Era As An Easter Holiday." *Guadalajara Reporter,* 10 April 2004.

———. 2015. "Old Chapala town hall gets new lease of life." *Guadalajara Reporter*, 29 November 2015.

———. 2016. "First lady opens renovated train station." *Guadalajara Reporter*, 1 April 2006, 1.

Palomar Verea, Juan. 1995. "Contra la amnesia tapatía: para recordar a Pedro Castellanos." *Minotauro*, núm. 2, Guadalajara, 31 mayo 1995.

———. 2014. "Pedro Castellanos, el urbanista." *El Informador,* 28 November 2014.

———. 2016. "La ciudad y los días - El pueblo de Chapala como patrimonio." *El Informador,* 3 August 2016.

———. 2017. "Juan Palomar y Arias: a treinta años de su muerte." *El Informador,* 6 September 2017.

———. 2018. "Para escándalo barraganesco, este sí vale la pena: el jardín del Mago en Chapala ahora en destrucción." *El Informador,* 9 August 2018.

———. 2019. "Esplendores de Chapala (y algunos ocasos)". *El Informador,* 8 June 2019.

———. 2019. "Chapala: primera de las cuatro casas que Luis Barragán hizo para sí mismo." *El Informador,* 10 July 2019.

Pareyón, Gabriel. 2007. *Diccionario Enciclopédico de Música en México.* Zapopan, Jalisco: Universidad Panamericana, 2 volumes.

Parmenter, Ross. 1983. *Stages in a Journey.* New York: Profile Press, 83.

Partida-Rocha, Fernando. 2016. "Diario de un snob," *El Informador,* 12 December 2016, 4-B.

———. 2017. "Diario de un snob: Sybille Bedford, genial autora de 'A visit to Don Otavio'", *El Informador,* 19 June 2017.

Purdy, Al. 1980. *The D.H. Lawrence House at Chapala.* The Paget Press.

Rispa, Raúl and Antonio Toca. 2003. *Barragan: The Complete Works.* Princeton Architectural Press.

Rogers, Thomas L. 1893. *Mexico? Sí, señor.* Boston: Mexican Central Railway Co.

Romero Gil, Juan Manuel. 2013. *El Boleo: Santa Rosalía, Baja California Sur, 1885-1954.* Centro de estudios mexicanos y centroamericanos. OpenEdition Books. https://books.openedition.org/cemca/376 [23 January 2019]

Schafer, Joseph (ed). 1940. *Memoirs of Jeremiah Curtin.* Madison: The State Historical Society of Wisconsin, 527.

Scott, Hester. 1966. "Over One Thousand Children to have Gift Sweaters." *Guadalajara Reporter,* 10 December 1966, 4.

Solano, Arllete. 2015. "Retoman arquitectura religiosa del tapatío Pedro Castellanos." *Milenio.* 3 Sep 2015.

Taylor, Lisa. 2018. "Old Orange County Courthouse." Blog post dated 10 August 2018 at Preserve Orange County.org https://www.preserveorangecounty. org/places/2018/8/9/old-orange-county-courthouse [27 April 2020]

Tello, Antonio. *Crónica Miscelánea de la Sancta Provincia de Xalisco.* Guadalajara, Jalisco: Ed. Font. 1942.

Terry, Thomas Philip. 1909. *Terry's Mexico Handbook for Travellers.* México City: Sonora News Company and Boston: Houghton Mifflin Co.

Tipton, James. 2016. "María Felix: The Fantasy of the World." Originally published at mexico-insghts.com; reprinted in *El Ojo del Lago,* Vol 23 #3 (November 2016).

Traslaviña García, María Dolores. 2006. *Guillermo de Alba.* Gobierno de Jalisco Secretaría de Cultura.

Tweedie, Mrs. Alec (Ethel Brilliana Harley). 1901. *Mexico as I Saw It.* New York:
    Macmillan; London: Hurst and Blackett, 249-250.
Valerio Ulloa, Sergio. 1996. "Empresarios en Jalisco durante la revolución
    (1910-1920)", pp 21-47 in *Estudios Sociales* (U de G), August 1996.
Venegaz Muñoz, Verónica. 2009. "La Casa Ochoa." *El Informador*, 16 Aug 2009, 4-F.
Vuilleumier, Fernanda. 2007. "Lake Chapala, Hacienda El Manglar". Post dated 6
    November 2007 at haciendaelmanglar.blogspot.com/ [31 January 2019]
Young, Virginia G. 1991. *A History of the American British Cowdray Hospital in
    Mexico City.* (The British in Mexico, number 6). Mexico City: The British
    and Commonwealth Society, 9-10.

Index

Acknowledgments

Given that this book has been more than two decades in the making, it is impractical to list everyone who has helped shape the final result. Nevertheless, I must single out certain individuals who have provided especially valuable support.

The staff of the Archivo Histórico Municipal de Chapala have been unfailingly helpful. My particular thanks go to the late Armando Hermosillo Venegas, who oversaw the archives from 2001 to 2006, Zaida Cristina Reynoso Camacho, who was in charge of the archives from 2012 to 2015, and to Rogelio Ochoa Corona, who has continued to promote the area's history via his web-based videos since managing the archives from 2015 to 2018.

I gratefully acknowledge the assistance of Michael Forbes and Sean Godfrey, who provided unlimited access to the archives of *The Guadalajara Reporter*, and Lic. Blanca García Floriano, coordinator of the Hemeroteca Histórica del Biblioteca Pública del Estado de Jalisco "Juan José Arreola," who helped facilitate access to early editions of newspapers published in Jalisco. In Ajijic, Marianne O'Halloran, the Lake Chapala Society archivist, and the Society's then executive director, Terry Vidal, graciously gave me free reign to explore its archives, including its Neill James collection.

Invaluable contributions, corrections and help have come from Dr. Ben Brown, Jim Brown, Arq. Fernando Brizuela, Martín Casillas de Alba, Ros Chenery (owner of Mi Pullman), Maricruz Ibarra, Katie Goodridge Ingram, Mona Lang, Jorge Varela Martínez Negrete, Dr. Marijane Osborn, Dale Hoyt Palfrey, Arq. Juan Palomar Verea, Fernando Partida-Rocha, and Jane Rees. Celia Burton kindly proofread the final draft. My thanks to each and every one of you; your assistance and encouragement have greatly improved this book.

I am especially grateful to Ing. Mario González García for allowing me to reproduce photos of postcards in his collection, and to Margarita Manzo viuda de González for permitting me the use of several photographs taken by her late husband, the long-time Chapala photographer José de Jesús González Miranda (1898–1995).

Finally, I could never have completed this book were it not for the unconditional support behind the scenes offered by my family.

Author

Tony Burton, born in the UK in 1953, is a geographer who taught, lectured and guided specialist cultural and ecological trips in Mexico for eighteen years.

He has written extensively on Mexico's history, economics, tourism and geography, and won ARETUR's annual international travel-writing competition for articles about Mexico on three occasions. His work has been published in numerous magazines and journals in Mexico, Canada, the US, Ireland and elsewhere. His previous books include *Western Mexico: A Traveler's Treasury* (fourth edition, 2014), *Lake Chapala Through the Ages, an Anthology of Travelers' Tales* (2008) and *Mexican Kaleidoscope: myths, mysteries and mystique* (2016). His cartography includes the best-selling *Lake Chapala Maps*, first published in 1996. Tony also co-authored, with Dr. Richard Rhoda, the landmark volume *Geo-Mexico, the Geography and Dynamics of Modern Mexico* (2010).

Tony and his wife, Gwen, live on Vancouver Island in Canada and revisit Mexico as often as they can.

Other books by this author

Western Mexico: A Traveler's Treasury (4th edition, 2014)

"One factor that lends special appeal to this singular travel book is Burton's departure from the stock formula found in conventional guides. He adheres to a more organic approach, drawing on personal experience and meticulous research to divulge the virtues and peculiarities of every destination."

—Dale Palfrey, *The Guadalajara Reporter*

Lake Chapala Through the Ages, an Anthology of Travelers' Tales (2008)

"Intermingled with the first-hand accounts of the area in different eras, Burton provides snippets of background history to give some larger context and enhance the reader's overall understanding of this particular region and Mexico in general.... Burton is a consummate scholar whose writing is also enjoyable to read."

—novelist Robert Richter

Geo-Mexico, the Geography and Dynamics of Modern Mexico (2010) (co-authored with Richard Rhoda, PhD)

"Geo-Mexico illustrates both the richness of geography as a field of study and the spectrum of cultural, economic, and environmental anomalies that make Mexico so eternally fascinating... I highly recommend this volume to educators, students, and anyone with more than a passing interest in the culture, history, terrain, economy, politics, or development of the country."

—Felisa Rogers, *The People's Guide to Mexico*

Mexican Kaleidoscope: myths, mysteries and mystique (2016)

"In this lively interweaving of history, cuisine, culture, tradition and superstition, Tony Burton brings the reader refreshing and often startling insights into the forces that shaped Mexican culture. There is something for everyone in this eclectic collection: from cross-dressing maids to miraculous births, from Aztec farming to the Manila connections... a suitable gift for the novice flying to Mexico for vacation and a cherished companion for the expat already comfortably at home there."

—author Dr. Michael Hogan